The Kindness Project

Chris Daems

Published by

The Endless Bookcase

Suite 14, STANTA Business Centre, 3 Soothouse Spring,

St Albans, Hertfordshire, AL3 6PF.

Cover artwork by Russell Daems

Paperback Edition

Also available in multiple ebook formats.

ISBN: 978-1-914151-64-4

Available from

www.theendlessbookcase.com

Dedication

Sophie, who makes me laugh (almost!) every single day. I'm excited to see the places you'll go and all the laughs yet to come!

Charlotte, my podcast partner in crime and travelling buddy. Thank you for being amazing.

Cassie, the woman who holds it all together. I love you.

Oh, and let's not forget...

'Producer Russ' – The podcast, or this book, wouldn't exist without you. I'm proud to call you both my brother and my friend.

About the Author

Chris Daems is a business owner, father of two and somebody who strives to make the world a better and kinder place.

In his professional life, he is a Chartered Financial Planner. However, one of his 'favourite hobbies' is as co-host (along with his eldest daughter Charlotte) of *The Kindness Project* podcast. Hosting the podcast has provided him with an opportunity to explore kindness in all its forms and interact with the people who are doing kind things in this world.

His optimism and positivity give him a unique perspective on the world and those within it. For the past five years, he has compiled an archive of altruistic achievements from across the world while sharing laughs and inside jokes with his daughter Charlotte and his brother, 'Producer Russ'.

The podcast, originating in the UK, has evolved into a community of listeners from across the globe and has been listened to in 164 countries across the world (all the way from Albania to Zambia).

Reviews

"This wonderful book has captured what it really means to be kind, and just how easy it is. It picks up and expands on some simple but truthful themes, and you can feel the pages radiating with the same infectious smile and sense of fun that makes *The Kindness Project* podcast so good. Well done Chris!" **David Forsdyke, Knight Frank**

"During reading this book I walked past a homeless man - 'any spare change' to which I said sorry no and walked on, then one of Chris' similar stories popped into my head. I went back and gave him the brownie I'd been saving. This is a book that makes you reflect on your own character and relationships, what it means to be kind to yourself and others. A warm, enjoyable, inspirational read, packed full of wisdom and actionable ideas. Chris is kinder than he knows, and it's a timely reminder for us all to be kind to ourselves and others. Once you start on the kindness journey, it's infectious!" **Keith Boyes, Spentwell**

"In *The Kindness Project*, Chris Daems gifts readers a brazenly honest and highly engaging account of his own quest to be kinder in life, with off-the-shelf lessons for the rest of us. In reading *The Kindness Project*, you'll be reminded of the joy that comes not only from simply being kinder, but in finding connection with another human being... something the last few years has shown us is critical to our own humanity." **Lauren Janus, Phila Engaged Giving**

"Overall I completely agree with the points raised in the book. I personally would struggle with some of the things suggested but the I fully support the basic premise in that the world would be a better place if we were all a little kinder.

"I'm also very interested in the concept of ethical investing. Something I'm going to discuss with Chris at our next meeting.

"As for abseiling or jumping out of planes. Not for me!

"Overall a short and concise review of how being kinder can make the world a better place, backed up by some interesting facts and science." **Mike Corder**

"For me, there are two things that need to impact me to make me want to immerse myself in reading a book - commonality and community. How does this resonate with me and how does this apply to me? Chris' storytelling instantly resonated with me and his insights around the subject of kindness was delivered in a non-fluffy, 'real' way that most people avoid. A must read!" **Nick Elston**

"I thoroughly enjoyed reading *The Kindness Project* and was sad for it to end. Thanks to Daems for sharing the collective wisdom gathered from years of podcasts and lessons about kindness and insights from his own life delivered with such honesty, heart and humour. This is a handbook and collection of notes from Daems' personal journey full of discovery, inspiration and nostalgia. It feels like Daems is in the room with you, sharing stories about his childhood, family, professional life and the many high, lows and laughter along the way. Read this book to learn about the science and benefits of kindness, and find practical ways to be kinder to yourself, others and even the planet." **Patrick Luong, GoodGym**

"The really inspiring and practical guide that we all need to bring a bit more happiness into our lives and the lives of others in these trying times. A funny, honest and informative read." **Sally McEnallay, Marketing Director, Greenkit**

"This is not a self-help book but you will help yourself by reading this book immediately! A lovely read that will fill you with kindness!" **Sam Chilton-Cox, Law Choice**

"I read it with interest and enthusiasm. Having had the pleasure of participating in *The Kindness Project* podcasts and with my work in health, mental health and overseas- this writing and the story speaks to our wellbeing, as humanity, on so many levels. Thank you for sharing your story with humour and accessibility." **Vasanti Hirani, Daal Bhaat Panni**

Foreword

Over the past few years I've enjoyed being part of an amazing project. Five years ago when this all began, my dad and I started out sitting in the garage at home with a microphone he'd bought especially for the podcast. Since then, this project has given us so much more than we originally intended.

The podcast was designed to share kindness in the world – but it has brought me enormous joy, as well as a treasury of special moments with my dad captured through the microphone.

When we started this journey, Dad was talking about writing a book for *The Kindness Project*. A collection of people, events and acts, that showed that there was kindness out there in the world. When I think about what the podcast was all about, I think back to one of the earlier questions of the podcast; are people generally good?

I remember being uncertain about this question, and even when we got to the end of our discussion in episode three, we never truly reached a conclusion. It is something that we continue to examine in each episode of the podcast. From what we have found, what we have shared, and what we have learned, I believe that people have a great capacity for good.

It has become a large part of my life, working with my family to create this wonderful little thing that grew far more than any of us could have imagined. It has become a beast of a thing that has connected with and touched more people than I can count.

Then there was lockdown. Covid-19 came out of nowhere and, suddenly, we couldn't leave the house, hang out with friends or even go into school or work.

Near the beginning, Dad introduced the idea to me of doing morning live sessions instead of our regular recording sessions. Most mornings, we would stream our little talks on a Facebook live, and later, the recordings of these lives would be released after editing.

Soon we added live guests joining us in the sessions, so I got to be involved in more interviews than I ever had before. It was wonderful to respond to the live comments and get an actual sense of engagement. Before we did the live shows, the idea that anyone would listen to these podcasts was a bit abstract and intangible. These live recordings gave me a focus in the mornings and were something that gave me purpose besides walking my dog, reading and thinking of what I would do when lockdown was finally over.

The Kindness Project has been a journey in many ways. While the podcast grew and grew, I was growing alongside, perhaps not at the same pace. I was just a teenager when the podcast first began and it has seen me through my teenage years and into my early adulthood. That is definitely a weird thing to say.

Now that I am living on my own for the first time, I cherish every recording session, each in-joke made, every intro and outro and slip of the tongue seem more weighted with meaning now that I don't have access to it as often. While I cannot be certain of how my dad perceives *The Kindness Project*, for me it started as an idea, it became fun times spent with my dad and since then it has even become an important aspect of my life that I am immensely grateful for.

While we were usually the faces, or rather voices, of *The Kindness Project*, we owe a lot of the podcast to Russell too, who looked after all the technical aspects. To anyone who has been listening to more recent episodes of the podcast, my uncle's voice can be heard a lot more. Not only does it add a third voice to the podcast, but it has also introduced even more to our recordings. But long before that, when he was our producer, he was adding so much to the content of the podcast, with his skills of editing and his organisation of a lot of the behind the scenes things that I am not even one hundred percent aware of. .I don't know if this podcast would have gone as well or run as smoothly without our amazing producer, Russ, managing things in the background while we shared our take on kindness with the microphone.

This book is amazing and I am incredibly proud of my old man for it. I have always known him to be a man of conviction. I have seen him push himself and work himself hard in pursuit of his goals. This year it seems that several of the goals that I have seen him strive for as I grew are finally coming to fruition. Not only has he managed to complete the book this year, but he has also attained another qualification, the highest he can achieve. And even as he completes these goals, he continues to set himself more that I know one day he will achieve (although I may be a little bit biased).

I hope you love this book as much as I do and, perhaps, you will join us on the podcast too.

~ Charlotte J Daems

Contents

Contents

Prologue

I'm not particularly kind.

I'm probably no kinder than you and certainly no kinder than the kindest person you know. However, in the last few years I've tried to be a little better; a tiny bit more understanding, a little bit more compassionate.

I want to be kinder.

This book is the story of what I've learned about kindness. I've done this by listening, by sharing the stories of people doing amazing things around the world on our podcast.

Oh, I haven't mentioned the podcast yet have I? I host *The Kindness Project* podcast with my daughter, Charlotte. It's close to both our hearts and has become an important part of our week.

But we're getting ahead of ourselves. Let's go back a bit; it's 1985 in a cold infants' school hall in East London. This is when I truly appreciated how important kindness was.

This school hall, like so many built in the late 19th century, was in a particular style - high ceilinged and brown bricked with natural light streaming through the windows.

The teachers and the pupils on the other hand were straight out of the eighties. They sported a lot of obscenely-patterned jumpers, a smattering of shell suits and a collection of massive hairstyles.

It was fun looking back at the old school photos, remembering the old teachers and grimacing at what I wore. Then I noticed in one of the photos a teacher was standing there, as proud as punch, who looks exactly like Stan Lee.

I don't remember him. It did make me wonder if Spiderman's creator was looking for inspiration for his next super-villain and decided to do a couple of terms as a teacher at an East London Comp.

There was no school uniform at the time, kids wore what they wanted. This meant the attire was a combination of casual sportswear, denims and a decent amount of wool. Looking back at the photos it seems that the more flammable the outfit the more popular it seemed to be.

Tuesday. 8:50am. School Assembly time.

As was typical at the start of an assembly there was a cacophony of noise as kids found their place in the hall. There was always a bunch of boys digging each other in the ribs. There was always the teacher who felt that yelling at the kids in their class would get them to settle down faster. There was always a kid running late and, in a rush to get to his place, stepped on the hands of at least half of the class.

The sounds faded and, apart from the occasional cough, the room was so silent you could hear a pin drop.

At the exact moment the headteacher stood, a loud noise echoed through the hall.

The offending noise making object wasn't a pin. It was Trevor, who had decided it was an appropriate time to throw his pencil case up against the wall. A giggle reverberated across the room and Trevor smiled broadly. Mrs Tritton, the headteacher, did the look. A look I'm pretty sure all teachers must learn at teacher training. That particular look on this particular day was laser-focused on Trevor and had the desired impact. The giggles subsided and Trevor's cheeky grim turned to stone.

It was a standard assembly in a lot of ways. There were the songs you heard in primary schools across England at the time. 'If I had a Hammer', 'Let it be' and a song called 'If I needed a neighbour'. This particular ditty had the line, "I was cold. I was naked," which, in a room full of primary school children, always generated a laugh.

There were a few announcements then, about three-quarters of the way through, it happened.

A teacher, whose name I fail to remember (although I do remember it wasn't Stan Lee), stood up at the front of the room.

"We've got a special announcement today. It's incredibly rare we do this but we'd like to present a very special child with a gift. Every break time this young boy sits quietly on a bench reading his book. However if he sees someone who needs help, or needs some support, he actively goes to help that person."

A quick cough and then she continued, "We've never done this before, but we've got something special for this particular pupil - a special award for kindness."

At this point I'm searching the children. Wondering who this amazingly kind superchild could be. Was it John? Or Terry? It definitely wasn't Trevor!

"So, can Chris Daems please come to the front?"

I remember the shock. Then the surprise. Not only that 'it was me', but also the fact that my face had very promptly turned from cream to crimson.

All eyes were on me as I wandered to the front and stood next to the teacher facing the entire school.

"We're got a special prize for you Chris just to say thank you."

I wondered in that second what it might be. Would it be a transformer, or an etch a sketch. It's probably going to be something more educational like a speak or spell.

"We're giving you -"

It might even be a Tomy-Tronic, or a game for my Commodore 64, or a bike!

"- a plate."

The plate in question was passed from one teacher to another. Then to me. I tried to look impressed. Don't get me wrong it was a lovely piece of crockery. Blue and white. A garden with two birds. Willows. Chinese in style. Just not something you want when you're eight years old or, come to think of it, forty-three.

I took my plate, thanked the teachers and sat down, embarrassed, but also a little bit proud.

I remember walking home wondering what would happen when I told my mum. I soon realised, as I turned the corner and could see our house, she already knew. I remember her waiting outside. I remember the smile on her face. I remember a hug. But most of all I remember her words…

"I'm so proud of you. Don't stop being you. Don't stop being kind."

I'd never felt better.

Thirty two odd years later I'm sitting in my mums flat. A few weeks before she'd got the news. It was lung cancer and it was terminal. I'm not sure at that point I'd come to terms with the news, but my mum was being practical.

She wanted to organise her funeral and knew the songs she wanted played and how she wanted to speak. She also had an idea of where she wanted her possessions to go.

She kept all her keepsakes in a wooden cabinet in the middle of her front room. This cabinet she told me contained good memories. Times we'd made her proud, school reports, little mementos that produced good memories. And hundreds of photos.

We were looking at an old photo. Mum looked happy and youthful with a broad smile across her face. Me, my brother Russ and my sister Kay all looked awkward in a outfits we'd clearly been forced to wear.

She smiled.

"That reminds me," she said as she headed to her keepsakes cabinet, "I've kept something for you, boy!"

After a couple of minutes of rummaging my Mum had found what she'd been looking for.

Blue and white. A garden with two birds. Willows. Chinese in style.

"Do you remember this?" she said smiling.

I smiled, but had tears in my eyes. "Yep."

"Do you want it back?"

"I do."

A few weeks later. My 16 year old daughter Charlotte and I are sitting on a bullet train bound for Tokyo.

We'd been planning the trip for a year and wondered whether we should cancel because my mum was so ill. My mum insisted we didn't.

That's when the call came.

My brother Russell with two simple words.

"She's gone."

I immediately looked at Charlotte and she knew - and there we were. An English dad and his teenage daughter, in floods of tears on a Japanese bullet train. Surrounded by Japanese salarymen who were looking rather confused and embarrassed.

After a few minutes of tears I was feeling a little calmer. Then, as I was looking out over the Japanese countryside, I found myself contemplating one memory.

That plate. The plate she'd kept safe for decades.

and then...

My Mum waiting at the end of our road for me to come home on that particular day. Her words that I'd forgotten, then remembered, but now would stay with me forever...

"I'm so proud of you. Don't stop being you. Don't stop being kind."

Introduction

The idea for *The Kindness Project* started in earnest in the Spring of 2016. Three decades after I'd received my blue plate. Three years before my mum would lose her life.

Looking back I wish I'd known we had so little time left. Three more years to spend some proper time with my mum. Three more years for my daughters to create memories with their nan. Three more years to drink my mum's awful cups of tea and listen to the stories we never knew were true or half made up.

Usually I'm not a fan of looking back, preferring instead to focus on what's to come. But every now and again I do wonder what I'd change if time was rewound and I had those three years again.

On this particular evening, the sky was dark and the bright spring sun had set a few hours ago on a balmy Saturday in London. I was hungry, tired and more than a little grumpy. Actually, a little grumpy is an understatement. I was a combination of Oscar the Grouch, the Grinch with a little bit of Gordon Ramsay's anger thrown in.

Walking, headphones on, I reached the road which I knew led to the entrance to a hospital. That's when the man approached me.

It was difficult to determine the age of the man - he could have been anything from fifty to seventy. It was dark and his head was down. One things for sure, he wasn't in great shape. He was walking with a limp, his hair was unkempt and dirty, his clothes ill fitting.

He slowly looked up and managed a half smile. Despite not being in the best mood I managed to smile back expecting nothing more. A smile between strangers forgotten as soon as it happened. But then something interesting happened.

The man lifted his head, looked me in the eye and started to speak.

"Excuse me pal. Can you help me out?" said the man, his eyes looking more melancholic than tired.

"I'll try," I said, not entirely meaning it.

"You see I'm just out of the hospital," said the man. "I've got nowhere to sleep tonight and I'm heading off to find somewhere to lay my head down. I usually sleep in the graveyard or on a bench. You couldn't do a fella a favour and help me out with a couple of quid."

My immediate reaction was typical. It was one I'd repeated hundreds if not thousands of times on the streets of London.

"Sorry mate, I can't help you," I said, "I haven't got any change." It was more of a reflex - a homeless man asks for money and this was my practised response.

In fact, I didn't have any change - I didn't have any cash at all. I did however have my bank card. A bank card which could have purchased a sandwich or a coffee from the Tesco I knew was two minutes' walk away.

But I didn't. The reflex response had already kicked in, I'd already said I couldn't help despite knowing I could have done SOMETHING. I'd lied.

I continued to walk down the road past the man. Then they both hit me. A simultaneous thought and a feeling.

The thought: "You know you could, and should, go back

and see if you can help."

The feeling: Guilt.

I stopped. Here this guy was. He clearly needed some help and I was in a position where I could deliver that help. What kind of fella would I be if I didn't even offer?

I turned around and realised that the man had continued walking after I'd rejected his request to help. I ran after him and as I approached he was picking up a cigarette butt off the floor.

"Excuse me, mate," I said.

The man jumped back startled.

"Sorry," I said, "I didn't mean to frighten you. I know I told you that I didn't have any change to give you. That was true. What I do have is my debit card - and if you wanted a coffee, coke or sandwich there's a Tesco two minutes up the road. I'd be happy to help."

The older man stood up a little straighter and smiled, his eyes still apologetic, "Can I have a beer instead?"

I was taken aback. I'd offered hopefully, but he'd said something I wasn't prepared to help with. Looking back I should have said 'no' and repeated my offer of a drink and a bite to eat.

I'm not proud of what I did next. I hope with hindsight if this ever happens again I'd try to do things differently. This time I took the easy route.

I mumbled 'sorry' under my breath and walked away, leaving this poor guy more confused than before.

To my shame I didn't look back. I walked away from this guy needing help for the second time that day.

Ten minutes later this particular encounter with this man started to bother me. I usually find walking quite a cathartic experience. One where time floats away as I simple focus on one step in front of the other. This time I had questions on my mind which wouldn't go away.

Why didn't I buy him a beer and a sandwich? What made you instinctively turn away again when he asked for alcohol? What's going to happen to him now? Why doesn't the hospital continue to look after him? Should have I taken the man back to this hospital to see if they could have helped? Could I have taken him to a shelter?

For a few weeks I couldn't get this short encounter with this man out of my head. It bugged me that despite my hunger, tiredness and mood I could have helped.

I spoke to my wife Cassie, the kids, friends and my dad about my meeting with this guy. A meeting that lasted minutes, but had continued to gnaw away at my psyche.

All the time, all the questions I asked myself led to one underlying question. One as much as wanted to I couldn't avoid -

"Why didn't you do more?"

Everyone I spoke to reassured me. They told me not to worry. They told me, despite knowing this not to be true, that I'd done all I could to help.

Then I found that I was asking myself some different questions.

Next time I see someone living on the street how am I going to react? What do I need to do to understand how I can help more? What do I know - REALLY know - about being a kind person? What can I do to become more kind?

You see I wanted to be better. I wanted to be thoughtful,

considerate, loving, generous and kind. I felt I wasn't doing enough. I also believed, and continue to believe, that most people are decent.

My acts of kindness were more likely to be accidental than intentional. I was a bit of a kindness Frank Spencer. Although the cat has never done a whoopsie in my beret. Probably because I don't own a cat - or a beret.

So, I wanted to be a little kinder - only a little. My aspirations were pretty modest; I wasn't aiming to be a kindness Superman or Spiderman. I was just trying to be a bit more of a modest kindness hero. Like Bananaman.

The catalyst to be kinder may have been sparked by that random encounter on an East London street. I suspect however the fuel to continue to be kinder came from somewhere deeper. The relationship with my two daughters.

For me being a dad is one of my primary drivers, but I've got to admit that it's the 'job' I'm most conflicted about.

On the plus side it's the thing in life which I love the most. The pride you feel when one of your kids does something special can't be beaten.

I love it when I hear my girls laugh, or do something that makes me proud, or achieve something that means so much to them. I also love it when they make me laugh, or make me think or challenge me to see life from their point of view.

But there is a flip side...

As parents you have this responsibility - the burden, amazing as it is, of guiding a young life. I became a father in my mid-twenties and was given this awesome responsibility.

You're responsible for guiding. You're responsible for nurturing. You're responsible for supporting this small human through their early years. All with no guide book. All while you're still trying to work out what good parenting actually looks like.

So, there's no parenting rule book. No instructions to this young human apart from lots of well-intentioned advice. No warning on the economic impact of having kids (why didn't someone warn me about THAT!). No choice but to try a lot, fail a bit and scramble towards the goal of having raised a functional human being or two.

We've got two girls and this comes with challenges. If you've got three kids or more you're clearly a glutton for punishment...

...and with all that said, it's still the best job in the world.

There's no denying parenting is challenging and draining. There's pressure to want to do your best and an unescapable reality that often your best isn't good enough. There's glimmers of hope that you're raising decent human beings. The challenge is this comes with the fear you might not be.

Despite all this it's still worth it. Being a parent can be amazing. Especially when you find out your child is funny, likeable, hard-working and kind.

The biggest motivator in my life are my daughters. You see I wanted to be a role model to my girls. To be someone who acted in a way they could be proud of. A good man. A kind man. Someone who succeeded, whatever that means, and did it in the right way.

The challenge I faced was that 2016 didn't feel like a year for kindness. Trying to be kind in 2016 felt like I was swimming against a cultural tide. At that time the world felt, to me anyway, a little crueller than ever before. Part of it was what was happening in the UK politically.

In the middle of the year in the UK the vote to leave the European Union was at the forefront of people's minds. Everyone had their own opinions, but an interesting thing happened.

The debate became polarised and, for many, it got much more personal, particularly online.

It seemed that you either sat in one camp or the other. Each side becoming more convinced they were right. You were either a 'Remainer' or a 'Brexiteer'.

As the debate roared on each side became more entrenched. Direct insults were thrown around like confetti. The debate became less respectful, less nuanced - definitely less kind.

On the other side of the pond another political leader had emerged who broke all the rules. A man famous for being famous and who used a clear skill for showmanship to great effect.

Donald Trump was direct and bombastic. His approach clearly popular with those who felt ignored by the mainstream. He talked about being different to career politicians who has spent too much time in 'the swamp'. He sold himself on his business experience.

During 2015 and 2016 Donald Trump's political power went from strength to strength. Through all the lies, scandals and controversy, more and more American citizens rallied behind his cause.

What bothered me the most about Donald Trump was the way he treated people. He chose to divide instead of unite. He insulted, he bullied, he took aim at the individual - not their ideas. It seems he would do, or say, anything to win. He'd never admit his mistakes.

As Trump grew more and more popular there were many who looked on in disbelief, including me. I wondered whether my view that the world was mostly full of decent people was naive.

I wondered whether the world had become less kind - and I was considering what to do about it in my own little way.

I decided to start on my own doorstep. How could I be a little kinder to myself? Then a little kinder to my community? Then a little kinder by fundraising for a couple of local charities?

As the autumn nights drew in I found myself losing motivation and inspiration. I've got a tendency in the autumn and winter months to start to hibernate, I get a bit more insular. Like a dormouse, if a dormouse lived in Essex and called himself Chris.

So I needed to take more action.

It's important to be clear. There are plenty of people kinder than me. People who are kind every day as part of their jobs. People who spend their majority of their time helping others.

For me I wanted to understand more about those people. The people who were the kindest among us. The individuals who, in a world which recently seemed less compassionate, had compassion by the bucketload.

I've always found that the easiest way to learn is to ask questions. However phoning someone up to ask them how to be kind felt a little strange. So I needed an excuse to learn more about kindness. A reason for these people to share their stories. A way we could use these stories to benefit them.

Then it hit me - we'd start a podcast. I'd host it with my

elder daughter Charlotte, who at the time was 14 and invite people on to tell their story. They could be from any country, any background, religion, race or creed, but they all had to have one thing in common - they must be doing something good in the world...

Now I appreciate 'good' is in the eye of the beholder. Like so much in our lives it's down to perspective. You might think a foot long subway sandwich is 'good'. I might think an eighty year old woman wing walking is amazing. You might feel better after a particularly satisfying burp.

However the criteria was clear. We'd interview people who did amazing stuff which benefitted others. Which benefitted the world. People who were proactive and active in their acts of kindness.

That 'doing good' might be to educate. It might be to inspire. It might be to support, or teach, or fundraise. Some of our guests have launched mobile apps used by millions. Others have started life changing charities. Others have helped people by building kinder workplaces. All of our guests have been amazing human being in one way or another. All of them have amazing stories to tell and insights to share.

Interviewing these people has changed me. I feel more optimistic about the world. Most inspired. More positive in the belief that most people are generally good.

One side benefit of recording the podcast is that I'm lucky enough to work with one of my favourite people in the world. My daughter Charlotte.

The interviews on our podcast are focused on sharing stories of people doing good. There's also a decent amount of time where Charlotte and I talk about anything and everything. There have been times where we've 'gone deep'.

There have been times where we've made each other laugh until we cry. There's been some strange conversational rabbit holes...

We've chatted about jazz, Muppets and Pompeii. We've discussed brown bread ice cream, earwigs and bus journeys. We've laughed at Knobbly knees. Chortled at the Hamburgular. Chuckled at the fact that I'm the proud owner of a niche Facebook group all about satsumas.

For those who are interested the *Satsuma Appreciation Society* is still live on Facebook. It's got two members. Me and my wife Cassie. Clearly there isn't enough appreciation for satsumas.

I've been close to tears when Charlotte has recited her poetry on the podcast. We've cried with laughter at the names 'Barry' and 'Beryl' at least four times. We've discussed everything from Japan, exams, feminism, omelettes and flirting.

Since late 2016 we've produced a show which has gone out every week without fail and gradually grown in popularity. Although if I'm comparing it with my Satsuma fan club it isn't a particularly high bar.

In the early days we struggled to get guests to come on and talk to us. Now we get emails from people who want to come on and tell us their story and promote their book. We've had tens of thousands of downloads and thousands more every month.

We've been voted one of the happiest podcasts in the world. We've popped up in the Philosophy and Comedy podcast charts. We still love doing it.

I'm still inspired by the stories I hear on the podcast and feel lucky that I get to share these stories. In this book I'll share what I've learned about kindness along the way...

We'll first talk about being kind to yourself and how to put your own 'oxygen mask on first'. Then we'll talk about the small things we can all do to become a little kinder every day.

I'll share what I've learned from my guests about using our time more effectively to help others. I'll then explore how we might choose to be a little more charitable.

At that point we'll investigate how we can choose to use our money for good. I also believe that we can all show we're kinder at work and will explore why I believe kindness is also important in business.

Along the way we'll talk about the science of kindness. How kindness makes us happier. Why we should think about kindness in a practical way and much more.

If I've written this book and if you aren't inspired to take some positive action I haven't done my job. If you read this book and choose not to be a little more kinder it's a wasted opportunity. I'd encourage you to take what you learn from this book and apply it today. And tomorrow. And for as long as you can until being a little bit kinder becomes an integral part of your life.

So, first before we start our journey through kindness together, let me say thank you. I know there's plenty of choices when it comes to how you spend your leisure time so I'm grateful for the fact that chosen this book. I promise you I've worked hard to make sure you'll enjoy it!

So, let's tell some stories and have some laughs. Let's learn about becoming a little more caring, loving and kind. Let's learn how doing this will improve lives - most of all yours.

Shall we begin?

Chapter 1
Be kind to yourself

If you've ever been on a flight you know the drill. It's after the bit where the cabin crew shows us how to get out of the plane if we need to. It's straight before we're told where our life jackets are kept. The attendant explains:

"If cabin pressure drops oxygen masks will drop down from the compartment above your seat. Be sure to put your mask on before helping others."

Thankfully I've never have had to use an airplane oxygen mask. Although I suppose it's a lot better than having had to use the lifejacket or, even worse, the whistle and torch!

The oxygen mask announcement always makes me think about kindness. Specifically - **how to be kinder to yourselves.**

A few months ago on a typical Sunday morning I was sitting on the sofa reading the paper. Charlotte came into the room tears streaming down her face. As a caring dad I asked her "What's the matter darling?"

At that point she mumbled something, then ran out of the room with tears streaming down her face and crimson cheeks. She stomped upstairs. Then I heard the noise every dad of a teenage daughter across the land must be used to by now - the slamming of a bedroom door.

As I've already said I can't pretend I'm a particularly good dad - although I try my best. When it comes to parenting, despite trying to get a little bit better for years, I'm still a rank amateur. I'm the parental version of Ann Widdecombe on Strictly, with Cassie my wife being Anton Dubeke. I try hard but without expert help I'd be useless.

The problem I have with parenting is the fact that as kids change the rules of parenting seem to change. I start off learning the rules of parenting draughts. Then suddenly we're playing chess, and then Cluedo, and then Uno. All at the same time.

When it comes to trying to parent teenagers, all too often I feel like I'm playing Jenga. A game which requires subtlety and a deftness of touch. Although on occasion it ends abruptly with everyone shouting and screaming. At least that's how it's ordinarily played in our house.

Unfortunately a deftness of touch or subtlety aren't skills I'm not particularly known for.

After a few minutes I went to her bedroom door, knocked timidly, and entered the room. Charlotte was curled in a foetal position on her bed.

"Do you want to chat?" I said and despite the tears, and being wrapped up in a ball, she nodded that she did. She unfurled herself and I sat next to her on the bed. We talked.

Exams were approaching and Charlotte was feeling the pressure. She had also fallen out with a friend. A friend who, in my humble opinion, expected a lot of Charlotte but didn't give much in return.

One of Charlottes greatest qualities, and she's got a decent number, is how much she cares. One of my greatest frustrations is how much she cares.

On the majority of occasions Charlotte puts other people before herself. It's an admirable trait. However I also wanted her to understand that sometimes you need to be kind to yourself so you can be kinder to others. At that moment I just couldn't find the words to help her.

This lack of linguistic expertise, while not an unusual thing, made me feel a little helpless. I wanted to support her with a kind word, give some sage advice which placed the challenges she faced into perspective. The only thing I could think of saying was a cheesy cliché. So cheesy it might as well have been covered in Cheddar, wrapped in Camembert and then dipped in a Fondue.

"Charlotte. When you get on a plane and the flight attendant talks through the safety procedures what do they tell you?"

"Put on your seatbelt."

"Yes - and?"

"Tell you where your life jacket is."

"Ok - and?"

"Show you the emergency exits..."

It was clear at this point I hadn't been specific enough.

"Yes, all that as well as telling you about the Oxygen masks. What do they tell you about the oxygen masks?"

"Erm, I dunno Dad - breathe deeply?"

"They do say that, Darling," I said my tone of voice betraying my slight annoyance

"But they also tell you something pretty relevant to what you're going through at the minute."

Charlotte stared at me blankly.

"What they say, Charlotte," I continued, "Is that, before you help anyone else, you've got to put your own oxygen mask on first."

Another blank stare.

"What I'm saying Charlotte is that, maybe, before being kind to other people, you need to be kind to yourself."

Charlotte smiled.

"You know what," I started, "I don't think anyone gets the balance right one hundred percent of the time. I know you're a generous person so you're always going to try to support other people. I also think you need to spend a bit of time trying to be a bit kinder to yourself."

Charlotte looked up with one question…

"How?"

"Not sure," I said trying to answer as honestly as I could, "but there are a few things you could try."

Luckily I'd learned a little bit about some of the techniques designed to help us be a bit kinder to ourselves. Some from books, others from getting real insight from our podcast guests and, of course, from personal experience.

I know there's plenty of ways to be kinder to yourself and in this chapter I want to share a handful that work for me. There's plenty of evidence showing these techniques are pretty effective. However, there's nothing like some expert help - that's why I asked Ruth Hughes to help me.

Ruth is a positive psychologist practitioner; she runs her own consultancy and coaching business and has been a kindness project guest. Ruth also happens to be one of my favourite guests due to her amazing insights.

I've interviewed Ruth twice now. On both occasions I've gained useful insights in living a life where I'm kinder to myself. I'm sure by reading her input into this chapter you will too…

So, with useful insights from Ruth, here are some of my tips for the most effective ways to be kinder to yourself.

Avoid comparisons

> *"Comparison is the thief of joy"*
> *Theodore Roosevelt*

Every single one of the billions of us rolling about on this rock is amazing and unique. However, often we find ourselves doing something which evidence shows isn't great for our mental health.

We compare ourselves to others

The challenge we've got as humans is that we're hard-wired to compare ourselves to others. Also we're not alone in the animal kingdom. One experiment involved two Capuchin monkeys. One I'm going to call Steve and the other I'm naming Alan.

Scientists conducted a straightforward experiment. They gave Steve a piece of cucumber for performing a simple task.

All Steve had to do was to give a stone (which was sitting in the cage) to the scientist. Steve seemed happy with this deal for a while. A stone for a cucumber slice. That was until his buddy Alan got involved.

You see Alan was performing the same task as Steve. He was happily collecting stones from his cage in exchange for a gift. However wasn't getting a piece of cucumber. Instead he was receiving a grape per stone.

At this point, and despite previously being happy with cucumber, Steve was now discontented. He decided that if his mate was receiving grapes, he wanted grapes too. So, when he noticed Alan was receiving a far superior snack he started throwing back the cucumber slices at the scientist.

Now, while I don't make a habit of throwing food at people, you can understand the reason for Steve's disgust. Many animals, including humans, believe that fairness is important. Using comparisons allow us to see whether we are treated fairly.

So comparison is part of us. It's evolutionary. It's what monkeys like Steve, Alan, you and I do as part of our daily lives. We're not going to stop making comparisons.

The problem occurs when we suffer from what psychologists call **Social Comparison Bias.**

On occasion these comparisons can be helpful. They can provide opportunities to learn and allow us to become more resilient. However, when negative emotions bubble to the top, if we perceive someone else's life to be better than ours, these comparisons are unhelpful.

Ruth has an interesting insight...

"Having a role model who can inspire you to see possibilities and to see a way forward is a positive thing. However, it's also really important to avoid making unhelpful comparisons.

When I've started to feel these unhelpful comparisons in the past I've tended to question what's making me feel this way. That normally allows me to put these comparisons into perspective."

The reality is that the comparisons we make with others are often unreasonable. They're based on what people show us of their lives, particularly on social media.

Most people (including me) usually want to show the best of themselves online. We avoid showing the world the boring, frustrating and challenging parts of our daily lives.

Think about it this way. When was the last time you posted a photo on social media of you on hold to your mobile phone company? How keen are you to post a photo of you not looking your best just after getting out of bed? I bet you're desperate to do a Facebook LIVE the next time you and your partner are having a blazing row right?

Of course not - and most of us choose not to do this. We want to show the best side of ourselves. We know this, but it's still difficult to avoid comparisons with other people's 'ideal' lives.

It's a strange paradox - and a difficult habit to shake.

When I spoke to Ruth about this she told me that one of the most powerful ways to prevent you feeling this way. A question, which will provide some much-needed perspective.

What are you grateful for?

I'm 44 so well past my prime. My once wrinkle free and youthful looks are disappearing faster than my hair. In fact, I've got a bald patch so large I'm sure you can see it from space. Now enjoying a 'quick drink or two' involves a two day recovery period.

I enjoy running, but I'm slow. Dave, a guy who does my local park run, is 22 years older than me and at least five minutes quicker over the course.

A couple of years ago I ran the Paris marathon. At mile 21 I had a call from my family who revelled in telling me how slow I was.

Apparently I was being beaten by both a fat bloke in a tutu and a man with an Eiffel tower on his head. I'm such a slow runner that, during the same race, I actually got attacked by a man with a baguette trying to cross the road...

There's plenty of people better looking, wealthier, better organised, and smarter. There's plenty of people who sing better - actually you'd be hard pushed to find someone who sang worse!

And I'm one of the luckiest people on the planet.

The reality it's likely that you're pretty lucky too. At the least I'm sure you've got a roof over your head. You've got enough to eat. You'll certainly have at least a handful of people who love you.

When you **really** think about it there's at least ten reasons to be grateful - and probably a lot more

Gratitude allows us to do something important; it changes our mental focus. It switches our attention from what's missing to what we've got. It allows us to focus on what's going well.

The things I'm grateful for is a long list. It includes doing work I love and have control over. It includes having pretty decent health. It includes the fact that I can enjoy great music, love great art, travel.

I'm also grateful for the ability to continue to learn, develop and grow. I'm grateful for the time I've got left on the planet, however long or short this is. Since I lost my mum I've been increasingly conscious that I should not take this for granted.

I'm grateful for all the simple stuff - reading a book, enjoying a morning cup of coffee, hugs.

I'm also grateful that I live in the 21st century with all of the world's knowledge at my fingertips. The ability to connect with people better than ever before - even cat videos on YouTube!

There are plenty of studies confirming the mental health

benefits of being grateful. So, be kind to yourself. Take some time on a regular basis to think about what you're grateful for.

Ruth shares an interesting technique (originally from Martin Seligman), called the 'three good things exercise' you can use to be a bit more grateful every day.

> *On a daily basis spend a few minutes at the end of the day answering the following question:*
>
> **What three good things have happened in the past 24 hours?**
>
> *It might be 'enjoyed the taste of a cup of tea' or sitting outside in the garden for 10 minutes or watching a funny video.*
>
> *This allows you to spend time every evening focusing on the positives in your day and not the negatives.*
>
> *This should generate positive emotions and ultimately make you feel better.*

Only worrying about what we can control

> *"There is only one way to happiness and that is to cease worrying about things which are beyond the power of our will"*
>
> *Epictetus*

Over 2000 years ago a man was born as a slave. A slave born to work, but with a kindly owner who allowed him to study philosophy.

He enjoyed thinking about life in all its forms. However very quickly he found himself fascinated with one particular branch of philosophy. Stoicism.

In his teens or early twenties he managed to gain his freedom. At this point he had to make a decision about what to do with his life. Clearly there was less career choice back then. You couldn't be a web designer, or a drone pilot, or an Uber driver two thousand years ago. Despite the lack of options the path was clear for this particular man. He decided to become a teacher, specifically a philosophy teacher in Rome.

He started his Roman school and began to teach Philosophy. Then a problem occurred; a problem called Domitian.

Domitian was the Emperor of Rome at the time. Popular with the people and his own army, but not a fan of Stoics. Domitian decided that banning stoic teachings in Rome was the thing to do. This meant that, soon after setting up his school, the man was out of business.

So, the man decided to move. He set up shop in Greece, at a place called Nicopolis.

The man taught, but didn't write many of his ideas down. Thankfully his students were a little more organised and started recording his ideas.

One of his disciples, Arrian, decided to collate some of the man's best ideas into a little book. A book filled with the man's best ideas, many of which have stood the test of time.

The name of this rather impressive gentleman was Epictetus. One of the great Greek and Stoic philosophers.

Epictetus was one of the philosophers who first taught us that it's not 'things' which make us feel a certain way. It's how we think about 'things'. It's why we can all feel SO differently about Ed Sheeran, or Toy Story 4, or spiders, or being cut up on the road.

One of the things we talk about on the podcast quite a lot is the work of the actor Nicholas Cage. You see, I'm not keen on the work of Mr Cage - and I don't really know why. However every time he pops up on my telly his face has the ability to annoy me in a way I don't fully understand.

It may be the fact that I've wasted too much of my life watching some of the absolute dross he has been in.

Nicholas Cage fans might wax lyrical about *Raising Arizona* or *Leaving Las Vegas*. They might argue that *The Rock*, *Con Air* or *Face Off* are stone cold classics. They might reference his Oscar, or Golden Globe. They might even mention, arguably more importantly, his Blockbuster entertainment awards.

I'd suggest that for a proper perspective on Nicholas Cage you need to look at a broader range of his work. Films like *Left Behind*, or *The Dying of the Light* or *Looking Glass*. Films with a rotten tomatoes rating so low you'd struggle to sell them on the 'whoopsie counter'.

So who is right?

The die-hard Nick Cage fan. The one who owns a wide range of Nick Cage merchandise including (and all this is real Nick Cage memorabilia):-

- A reversible sequined cushion with Mr Cage's face on

- A T shirt emblazoned with a photo of Nick Cage as the Mona Lisa

- A mug covered with images of Nicholas as a Pizza.

Or me. A man who doesn't rate Nicholas Cage as an actor, doesn't rate a lot of his films and can't understand why people rate him so highly. Although even I'm considering a Nick Cage sequined cushion (I'm only human!)

The answer is neither.

It's all perspective. It's all about how we feel about the particular subject.

This applies to everything in our lives - our musical tastes, our political preferences, our reaction to other people's behaviour.

This may seem obvious. We all treat different things in different ways. However, this fact also reveals one underlying truth - one our philosopher friend Epictetus was painfully aware of. Ultimately we're responsible for our own opinions, attitudes and actions. There's no right or wrong when it comes to these things.

Everything is perspective.

Epictetus understood this and also argued that our time, effort and energy should be focused on one thing...

What we can control.

In our lives the majority of things are completely beyond our control. Whether it'll snow or your football team wins at the weekend. Or whether your favourite box-set pops up on Netflix. Or the majority of what we see on the news.

There's also the things we have influence over. Like the opinions of our family and friends or how well we do at work.

The stoics suggested that we need to be careful with our precious (and arguably finite) mental energy. Therefore, we need to spend our time and energy on the stuff we can change.

In fact, the short book of Epictetus's teachings starts with the following phrase:

"Of things some are in our power, and others are not."

And he continues, "Make the best use of what is in our power and take the rest as it happens."

So, to be kind to ourselves, we need to take the advice of a 2000 year old bloke and focus on what we can control.

If you're having a little chortle to yourself, you're probably not alone. You might argue that Epictetus knew little about modern life. Therefore his simplistic approach has very little to teach us about how to live today.

However, there is up-to-date research that tells us that focusing on what we can control does have a direct and positive impact on our lives. Back in 2014 a study taught the principles of Stoicism to a number of students. The results showed that focusing on what you can control has a positive impact on our lives.

The students found that their life satisfaction increased by 27%, Positive emotions increased by 16% and negative emotions reduced by 23%.

Ruth agrees - "Focusing on what we can control and what we can't is a really important part of building resilience. We've only got a finite amount of energy. So putting all of your energy into worrying about the things you can't control means one thing. It means the energy you spend on the things you can change is less."

Ruth continues by talking about a useful tool. One she learned from Steven R Covey's *7 Habits of Highly Effective People*. "Stephen Covey talks about the circle of control and circle of concern. This useful technique is to take two pieces of paper and draw two circles. You'd then write 'Circle of Control' above one and 'Circle of Concern' above the other.

"On the circle of concern page write all the things you worry about but can't change.

"On the circle of control page write all the things you can influence of change.

"Once you've completed both pages take the 'circle of concern' page and throw it in the bin. Then take the 'circle of control page' and decide what action you're going to take on each of the aspects of your life you have control over."

I like this idea. It's the physical manifestation of throwing away the worry and, while this might not work for you, there's no denying one thing. Focusing on what we can control, and ignoring what we can't is certainly a way we can live healthier, happier and more productive lives.

Making mistakes is fine - and forgiving yourself is even better

September 2019. Gibraltar airport. 9:42 pm.

My Dad and I step out of the small terminal building. Our destination is the short cab rank outside the airport.

We were both tired. While a flight from London to Gibraltar only takes a couple of hours we were both ready to hit the hotel and freshen up.

I assumed, due to the flight times, we'd want a quick trip to the hotel. With this in mind, and due to the fact that I'd spent a decent amount of time planning this weekend away, I knew that the hotel was only a 5 minute taxi drive away.

You see when I usually plan trips I'm pretty thorough. I read the reviews, I do my research, I got myself a guide book and I work out travel times.

I'd also picked the most Gibraltarian name for a hotel ever...The Hotel Gibraltar.

A taxi arrived and keen to head off I jumped in the front

and showed the driver the details of the hotel. He spoke one word loud and clear "No."

"Pardon," I replied "Why not?!"

"This hotel," the driver responded in a strong baritone, perfect English with a slight Spanish lilt, "is not in Gibraltar."

That's when the feeling started to hit me. The physical manifestation of the blood draining from my body. I hadn't booked a hotel in Gibraltar. I'd booked a hotel just across the border - in Spain.

In my defence the hotel WAS called the Hotel Gibraltar. It was so close to Gibraltar you could throw a stone and hit the Rock. It was just in another country!

We had to get out of the cab. Walk over the border. Thankfully there was a queue of taxis waiting on the other side. None of which we could use. You see, as I'd assumed we'd spend all of our time in Gibraltar I only had pounds sterling. Over the border in Spain taxis took Euros..- which meant a walk to our hotel. It's fair to say my 72 year old Dad wasn't happy.

I felt like an idiot and there's no denying that the act of making mistakes is a painful process. Even the most minor mistakes can make us feel ashamed and embarrassed. When we make mistakes it provides our inner critic with the chance to do what it does best.

However, we could look at the mistakes we all make a little differently. We might choose to look at the errors we make as a way to be a bit kinder to ourselves.

We can all self-criticise. We can all blame ourselves. Most of us are pretty good at doing this.

If we change the way we look at our mistakes they can be a

learning experience - a way to improve. Mistakes are inevitable; we all make them. But they can be useful depending on what we do when we err.

Ruth has an interesting perspective on making mistakes as she explains. "I think it's very difficult to learn if we don't make mistakes. When I was a teacher I used to say that talking about your mistakes is a gift to everyone in the class because of what we learn from them.

"The desire to be infallible and perfect is damaging to everyone because it's so unrealistic. We all make mistakes. It's often how we learn. However, it can also lead to fear, decision paralysis and an avoidance of making choices that might move our lives in a positive direction."

Thankfully there's plenty we can do to ensure we're being a bit kinder to ourselves when we do make mistakes.

Firstly it's important to understand that when you make a mistake it doesn't define you as an individual.

Secondly when things go wrong the healthiest way of dealing with a mistake is by admitting it, not blaming someone else for your error.

Every time you make a mistake, you can choose how to react.

We've seen, in recent years, the impact of Trump and his inability to admit his mistakes. Regardless of whether you agree with him politically or not, his inability to admit to his mistakes has been a major downfall for him. Time will tell how Trump is judged. However I do wonder whether the history books may have been kinder to Trump if he could admit his errors a little more openly.

Compare this to his predecessor, Barack Obama, who was clear on his opinion about making mistakes,

> *"You can't let mistakes define you.*
> *You must let them teach you."*

I know who I consider a more capable leader - how about you?

It's always worth talking to someone you trust about your mistake. Talking potential errors through with someone else allows us to relieve the pressure a bit. It also allows us to get another perspective and other potential solutions to this particular problem.

When we make a mistake it's easy to fall into the downward spiral of self-blame. This is not productive as it doesn't address the problem and just makes us feel bad. The important thing is to take the time to apologise, if necessary. Then take action to fix the issue.

On that particularly fateful night we had a long-ish walk to our Spanish hotel. We eventually arrived at the hotel and I looked at my dad. His face was a bright shade of crimson, but I couldn't decide if it was either anger or exhaustion from the walk.

"I'm sorry," I said to the old man, "but I genuinely thought this hotel was in Gibraltar. But let's look on the bright side - we'll be traveling internationally every day!"

He didn't laugh, or smile. It was too soon. However after a little while we realised it wasn't going to be a big deal and we enjoyed our trip.

One things for sure, I learned a lesson - keep an eye on international borders when I plan my future travels!

Choose what you consume

One of the best things about my dad is that he is normally

pretty supportive. When things have gone wrong he's there for a chat. He's also pretty good at encouraging me when trying something new.

I believe that knowing someone, or a few people, who have your back makes a difference. It removes some of the fear of trying new ideas and certainly knowing my dad is there to support me made a big difference.

However when I started *The Kindness Project* podcast his reaction was, erm, a little less enthusiastic.

"I don't get it Chrissy. What's the point of that?"

I tried to explain. In a world which feels increasingly polarised. In a world where the majority of the news was negative. I believed it was important to share more stories of people doing amazing stuff in the world.

"I know….but kindness. Who wants to hear about that?"

My dad might be right. Apart from a handful of exceptions the majority of the media we consume is focused on the negative aspects of our lives.

Crime, death, destruction, violence and mayhem are all common themes. Politics at its most contentious is another. There's not a lot of kindness going on.

Let's not pretend that good news is popular - we all know bad news sells. Psychologists call this negativity bias.

We remember traumatic experiences more viscerally than positive ones. We remember insults better than praise. Negative news attract our attention more than the positive stories. It's no surprise then that the media, in a desire to entertain and inform, focus on the negative in our world.

However, this isn't a true reflection of reality. ~In fact, most of our lives are full of the positive. The normal for many of us is human kindness. The normal for many of us is working together. The normal for many of us are far more examples of good than bad.

It's one of the reasons we don't hear more positive things in our world. In the words of the legendary Welsh octogenarian (Sir Tom Jones) - It's not unusual.

I'm not saying there isn't an appetite and audience for good news - and there are examples of how the media, both traditional and social, showcases good work.

Examples include the Community hero awards and Pride of Britain and days where many of us get together around a cause to give our support such as Red Nose Day, Stand up to Cancer and Children in Need.

However, the reality is that humans have evolved to focus on the things that potentially threaten us. Part of our attraction to bad news is the need to be aware of the potential threats in our lives - and this is the reason Journalists focus on the negative over the positive.

We've evolved to focus on danger and threat. This was critical when we shared our environment with wild animals, roaming the plains hunting and gathering meant always being ready for danger was a good thing.

Consider this; we've been evolving to avoid risk for millions of years. According to evolutionary scientists, our ancestors have been around for between 5-7 million years, but our evolution into anatomically modern humans only took place about 130,000 years ago.

The move from a hunter gatherer society to a farming society happened in the neolithic revolution, about 11,000 years ago. This then evolved into the modern societies we live in today.

In our millions of years of evolution and the majority of our history as Homo Sapiens we've had to be acutely aware of risk, danger and the potential threats, so it's understandable that bad news sells. It's our evolutionary selves thinking we need to be aware of the dangers.

However whilst this attitude might have served us well for the past few million years, therefore it's understandable that we've developed this focus on the negative; it's our chimp brain telling us we need to protect ourselves. I suggest that a constant and consistent focus on our threats and fears might not be the most appropriate way to deal with modern life.

There's plenty of evidence showing that being more selective about the content we consume has a positive impact on our mental health.

It's important to be informed about what's happening in the world, so I'm not suggesting that you ignore the news. But having a more active filter on what you consume allows you to be a bit kinder to yourself.

There are many ways you can control your media consumption more carefully. However, let me put all of my cards on the table; I know the negative impact of too much bad news and I'm still guilty of consuming way too much. I do use a few tricks to make sure my consumption isn't having a negative impact.

Firstly, I try to restrict the amount of time I spend watching the news. Instead of watching the news whenever it's on I actively choose that I'm going to watch, say, 20 - 30 minutes a day to stay informed - and no more. This isn't necessarily easy, but it is possible.

Secondly I try to manage my environment. I put do not disturb on my phone. I choose when to engage on social media, or the news. For me it's been both the simplest and one of the most effective ways of managing how and when I interact with the doom and gloom brigade.

Lastly, I intentionally focus on balancing the negative with the positive. I do this by intentionally seeking out those good news stories and looking for the news stories that represent the world we actually live in more fairly.

For me, there's no better place to start doing this than at the website Gapminder.org

Gapminder is a project started by Swedish doctor Hans Rosling. It's now run by his son Ola and daughter Anna after Hans's death in 2017.

The website is designed to highlight facts which allow us to build an accurate view of our world. Gapminder, for me, does an amazing job at being a source of counterbalance. A collection of facts which don't sugarcoat or ignore the underlying issues, but provide useful perspective.

In the book, *Factfulness,* written by the original founder of Gapminder, Hans Rosling, shares his insights. It's probably one of the most optimistic fact-based books I've ever read.

The big message is that, despite what we're told, the facts are that life, for most of us, has never been better.

- Airplane flight has never been safer

- Global life expectancy has never been longer

- Global wealth has never been greater

- In the past 50 years the number of individuals undernourished in the world has plummeted

- In the past 20 years extreme poverty has almost halved

- Child mortality has never been lower

- There's never been greater access to water, or electric, or access to the internet.

- Worldwide literacy is going through the roof.

While Gapminder, being fact based, doesn't ignore the issues we face as society, it does one thing well - provides us with data. This gives us an informed perspective on the world; a perspective which is often surprisingly positive.

So, if you're ever feeling the world is going to hell in a handcart, I'd suggest you visit Gapminder and take their quiz. I'm confident you'll find that the world is probably in a far better state than you think.

Healthy exercise

I'm certainly not what you'd call a natural athlete. At school I was one of those kids who was picked last for football. This meant that my position on the pitch was normally where I did least damage. Normally this wasn't in goal but somewhere on the wing. The reality was I was usually so far from the ball I might as well have been watching the match from home.

In my late teens I did make a conscious effort to become fitter, but this slipped in my mid-twenties and thirties. The fact that I had a busy working life contributed. I think the fact that our local Greggs was next door to my office didn't help.

However, in the last few years I've made exercise an integral part of my routine. This is for a bunch of reasons.

Firstly, I like the feeling. I enjoy feeling stronger, fitter and subsequently more confident. Also being more physically capable helps me to be more mentally fit. The mental health benefits of exercise are well documented. It reduces stress, produces endorphins which elevate mood and combats depression.

Many of us, before exercising, go through that period of dread. We think about the sweat, the pain, and the tiredness. The truth is that exercise as part of your daily routine makes us more energetic and helps us be happier.

There's also plenty of support you can plug into, from classes at your gym to couch to 5k programmes to lessons and classes in everything from Aerobics to Zumbe and much more.

So, if you want to be a little bit kinder to yourself get a little bit more physical exercise in your life. You won't regret it.

A growth mindset

It's 2018 and I'm sitting in my office. A couple of gentleman stroll through the door. One I recognise as Dave who runs the library our office sits on top of. The other man I recognise, but can't place immediately.

"Chris. I wanted to introduce you to Bobby."

The Bobby in question is a lovely fella called Mr Bobby Seagull.

Bobby (according to his Wikipedia page) is…

> *A mathematician, teacher and writer. Bobby appeared on University Challenge. He is also the presenter of the TV show "Monkman & Seagulls Genius guide to Britain"*
>
> *His first book is the life changing magic of Numbers.*

Bobby is super nice. Super smart. Super down to earth and, despite being busy with media work, continues to actively teach.

After a quick chat with Bobby, I was fortunate enough a couple of days later to introduce him at our local book festival. So, a couple of days later Charlotte and I went along to hear Bobby speak about his life, his work and his book.

About half an hour into his presentation he said, "I want to talk a bit about Mindset. Specifically about Growth Mindset and the work of a professor called Carol Dweck."

Now I'd read the book *Mindset* by Carol Dweck. If you're interested in how to be a bit kinder to yourself I'd suggest it's worth you doing the same.

To summarise Professor Dweck's research indicates that there are two basic mindsets which shape our lives. Fixed and Growth mindsets.

Fixed mindset people believe that intelligence (or aptitude), by and large, are fixed. A fixed mindset person might say "They're smart" or "Some people are natural singers - I'm just not one of them," or "I'm rubbish at Maths."

It's typical that someone with a fixed mindset believes that it's unlikely that you'll get better at something if you're not naturally skilled at it

A growth mindset person might say "They work hard" or "I had to learn how to sing" or "Becoming good at maths will be a challenge" Typically a growth mindset person believes in the capacity to learn new skills and the power to positively change your life.

Generally people with a fixed mindset give up more easily when faced with a challenge and take failure personally,

and

People with a growth mindset have a belief that they'll eventually learn and retain the knowledge or skills they need. That's why they stick at it and manage to achieve success when individuals with a fixed mindset might fail.

It's certainly worth reading Carol Dwecks book on this subject as it's massively insightful.

The evidence points towards those having a growth mindset being on the right side of history. The science points to being able to develop almost any skill, knowledge or talent. While natural talent might still be a contributing factor, its impact pales into comparison with simple hard work.

However, the evidence also points to the fact that people with a growth mindset are generally happier and calmer.

Interestingly one of the ways the NHS recommends we maintain positive mental health is by learning a new skill. Learning new things helps us develop our confidence. It also gives us a sense of purpose and, if done with others, improves our social connections.

Ruth agrees that a growth mindset is fundamentally important

"One piece of research showed how we can actively rewire our brains involved London cab drivers. As part of their training they need to have a deep and detailed understanding of London roads, known as 'the Knowledge'.

"The research found that as they learned the roads of London, their brains physically changed. The research found that cab drivers brains physically changed while going through this training.

"I'd suggest," Ruth continues, "that skills and strategies are always learnable. The evidence tells us this."

One thing which can put us off is failure and this is where Carol Dweck's findings come into their own.

Carol Dweck suggests that we remember that everyone we know who we consider an expert has failed thousands of times. These experts have learnt that this failure is simply learning in disguise.

Remember that with practice we get better. Nature might have gifted us with natural talents, but the evidence still points to the fact that practice contributes more to true experts than being 'a natural'.

I'd humbly suggest that, if you do want to be kind to yourself, pick up a copy of Carol Dweck's book. If it changes your perspective, just a little bit, it'll be one of the best purchases you'll ever make.

Connect, share and ask for help

On the west coast of England, further north than Manchester or Preston or Liverpool, sits a small coastal seaside town. It's also the origin of a relatively popular phrase we all use...

The town in question is probably more famous for potted shrimps, the home of a comedy legend or the Art Deco designed Midland hotel. It's not famous for this particular phrase.

The place is Morecambe and in November 1931 this phrase was recorded for the first time ever in the local paper.

"A problem shared is a problem halved"

There's plenty of research telling us that simply talking about our challenges helps. It's been shown time and time again that it relieves the stress caused by these problems.

Research by Age UK said that over a third of people feel brighter as a result of sharing their problems. Another quarter feel relieved that they have shared their problem. A further 8% feel that their problem disappears once it's shared.

The challenge we face is that, while attitudes are slowly changing, many of us have been taught not to share the challenges we face. A quick Google search of "Should I share my problems?" illustrates the issue that many of us face.

One of the first links which came up was for Quora, a website designed so that people can ask and answer questions. Normally Quora is pretty insightful. It answers questions such as

'What are the most surreal places to visit?'

'What can I learn or know right now in 10 minutes which will be useful for the rest of my life?'

All the way through to the frankly bizarre.

'Why didn't Batman ever need to answer nature's call while out crimefighting?' (Although, to be fair, it's something I'm now wondering about.)

However when answering the question about whether a problem should be discussed the advice from the website was less than great.

'Remember except your parents… no one gives a F*** about your problems. Only a few of your friends may bother about your problems, but after a certain time you will be mocked by them for facing such problems. When you are alone and feel like crying do that instead and at least you can relax for a certain time.'

Erm, OK.

I get it. This is some random thread on some random

website. It's the rantings of an anonymous person on the web. However, it does make me wonder how many of us share this particular opinion.

The reality is that we should ask for help as this not only means we feel supported, but it helps deepen the relationships we build with family, friends and at work.

There's plenty of research showing that we should be more vulnerable with people we trust. It also shows that asking for help and showing we're fallible every now and again makes us happier.

I get it. Asking for help means admitting you might not have all the answers. It requires us to be vulnerable, ignites our understandable fears of both being rejected and looking weak. However, the truth is that actually asking for help can strengthen any relationship. The best and most prominent example of this psychology principle in practice came from a man more famous for attaching a key to a kite in a thunderstorm, Mr Benjamin Franklin.

As well as being a prominent scientist Ben Franklin had a diverse range of talents. He was a writer, inventor, statesman, one of the founding fathers of the United States and a political philosopher. So it's fair to say Franklin was pretty influential. However, I believe the lesson we can learn from him, which is particularly pertinent in modern times, comes from a story in Benjamin Franklin's autobiography.

When he worked in local Pennsylvania politics, Ben was having a particularly tough time building a decent relationship with one of his political rivals. It was clear that the other chap wasn't keen on Franklin, but Ben felt that getting on a better footing with this particular fellow was probably a wise thing to do.

So, Franklin did something interesting. He asked for the

man's help.

You see the man owned a particularly rare book and Franklin felt a good way to develop the relationship was to ask the man if he could borrow the book. Wanting to help, and to be seen to help, the man lent Franklin the particular tome.

A week later Franklin returned the book with a thank you note and the next time the two men met the frosty relationship seemed to have thawed. All because Franklin had asked a favour of the other man.

Franklin told the story in his autobiography concluding that:

> *"He that has once done you a kindness will*
> *be more ready to do you another, than he*
> *whom you yourself has obliged."*

The story has sparked plenty of modern research into '*The Benjamin Franklin Effect*'. This shows that asking for someone help doesn't create a burden for the other person, but, in fact, deepens the bonds with that individual and the modern research validates Franklin's original assumption.

So, it turns out Franklin was spot on and the random cynic on the internet was wrong (I'm sure you knew that already!). Asking for help is scary, but the research proves that it's an excellent way to build a stronger relationship. We're social animals. We've evolved to help each other even though many of us do live in more individualistic societies than ever before.

So to be kind to yourself - ask for help. Find people you can connect with. You might find that the people you trust have the solution. You might find that they don't, but by talking it through you find the solution you need.

Do something kind

I often half joke on the podcast that being kind to others is incredibly selfish. The reason? It's been shown that being kind to others is amazingly good for our own mental health. It creates positive feelings, gives us a feeling of purpose and self-worth and helps us connect with other people.

Every time we witness an act of kindness a chemical reaction happens. Oxytocin is produced in our body. This boosts our mood and self-esteem.

Not only does Oxytocin get released we also get a hit of Seratonin. Seratonin is a hormone which makes us happy and keeps us calm. Also it's been shown to heal our wounds more quickly - in the unlikely event your act of kindness has resulted in an injury!

So being kind to others is also being kind to ourselves. It improves our health and reduces our blood pressure. It lowers stress and anxiety. It improves our emotional wellbeing and make us happier people.

So, if you want to be kind to yourself be kind to others. Not only will it make the recipient of the kind act feel better, it'll also make you feel amazing.

You can be kind in a bunch of ways and the remainder of this book will give you some inspiration to do this. It's a virtual smorgasbord of kindness ideas. A pick 'n' mix of kindness concepts; a tapas of thoughtfulness; a meze of compassionate acts.

Time to abandon my demonstration that I am skilled in metaphors, let's get on with it! In the next chapter I'll share some of the small things you can do to start to become kinder today.

Chapter 2
Everyday kindness

When I originally started to explore the world of kindness and was trying to understand how I might become a kinder person, I took the approach that made the most sense to me. I looked for what I could read on the subject - it's probably fair to say I've got a little bit of a book habit. I get so many books delivered I know my Amazon delivery driver's full name, birthday, kids names and favourite ice cream.

If you put 'kindness' into your favourite book retailer of choice you'll find a few amazing publications on the subject. One of these tomes is written by a lady called Bernadette. She is a writer, theatre maker and long-time resident of Deptford in south-east London and author of a number of books including *The little book of kindness*.

Bernadette also co-wrote and starred in a theatre show about kindness. The first few minutes being the funniest opening of a stage show I've ever seen. In this opening Bernadette, often in granular detail, describes all of the times she's been unkind in her life. It's hilarious and a great start to Bernadette's story on how she started her particular journey to be kinder.

However, five minutes into the show, after the hilarity of Bernadette's previous kindness faux pas, the mood suddenly changes...

Images of the 2011 London riots flood the screen on the stage and Bernadette explains how this for her was the flashpoint. She decided to take action to make the world a kinder place.

She went on a mission to spend a year performing an act of kindness to a stranger every single day. This has never stopped and for a number of years now she's performed at least one act of kindness each and every day.

Throughout this chapter we're going to be sharing insights from Bernadette as we explore what we can all do to make the world a better place one tiny step at a time using acts of everyday kindness. Let's start with an act you can do without even leaving your house…

Be kinder to the ones you love

Hopefully you're not like me. In the past I've been guilty of taking the people I love the most for granted and there's certainly one person I've taken for granted more than anyone else in my life. I see her every day. We're partners in business and in life. I love her today more than ever. Yet I've been guilty of not appreciating the amazing things she does as a mum, as a wife, in our business and much, much more.

When I started thinking about kindness and, in particular, when I read Bernadette's book, it got me thinking about how I'd treated my wife Cassie over the years.

I'm sure I'm not alone in saying this, but I'm sure there have been periods of our lives together where I've taken her for granted. It's certainly nothing to be proud of, but I suppose it's easy to get complacent about your closest relationships.

After all, *what's the point of telling someone how much you appreciate them, or giving them a compliment every day if they already know?*

What's the point of making someone breakfast in bed if they can make their own breakfast and you don't need all the crumbs in the bed?

What's the point of 'date night' when you spend so much time together anyway?

Reading Bernadette's book snapped me out of my complacency, and I vowed to be kinder to Cassie.

I WAS going to tell her that I appreciated her.

I was going to carve out time for us to spend together, and make sure we had a 'date night' at least once a month.

I was going to do a few more chores and make Cassie breakfast every now and again (although I did draw the line at 'breakfast in bed' as I reasoned that crumbs in bed are annoying and the bedroom is probably the least practical room to eat a full meal, apart from perhaps the small downstairs toilet).

Now I'm still a million miles from perfect. When it comes to being kind to Cassie my aspiration is to reach the summit of Everest and I don't think I'm at base camp yet, but something interesting has happened. Just being conscious of the fact that I could probably do a bit more means that I do. I'm certainly not going to win any husband of the year awards, but making a bit more effort in our relationship has made both Cassie and I a decent bit happier.

There's something arguably more powerful that I've also been a bit more conscious of since starting the podcast, reading loads and being increasingly curious about how we might be able to be kinder to the people we care for the most.

The power of three little words

I have a photo in a frame in my front window. It's of me,

aged nearly 5, dressed as a clown. Holding my hand and guiding me down the road is my cousin, Louise. She's a few years older than me so someone I've looked up to for a long time.

Louise is deeply impressive in lots of ways. She's a former karate champion, in her late teens she left London and moved to the island of Jersey to start a new life, she's an amazing mum, respected as a professional and one of the most emotionally intelligent people I've ever met.

One of the things I love about Louise is her ability to connect with people. She remembers things about you you've forgotten you've told her and always seems to find a way to be complimentary, funny and self-deprecating at entirely the right times.

One thing Louise is amazing at, and something I certainly didn't do often enough, is tell people she loves that she actually loves them.

It's so simple. Three little words.

I Love You.

Yet when I was thinking about how I could be a kinder person I neglected the importance of those three simple words. You see it's rare I uttered them.

Now I could make excuses. I could argue that the people I love know I love them so the words don't need to be said. I could tell you that I'm just not the type of person to say 'I love you'. I could say I'm just not naturally romantic, or emotional, or good at expressing my feelings.

We could debate the fact that saying 'I love you' too much dilutes the power of just three words, or by saying it too much to too many people you can't really mean it. It's an emotional risk for certain. However, the reality is that when

I started thinking more about my own particular journey to be a bit of a kinder bloke I realised that one of the things I could do is use three simple yet powerful little words way more often and certainly to the people I love the most.

What I found myself doing rather strangely is overcompensating and going from someone who didn't fell his wife and daughters he loved them at all through to someone who probably said it a bit too often.

This didn't go unnoticed by my family who thought this was hilarious and proceeded to give me a bit of ribbing for seemingly finding the ability to find my sensitive side, presuming that I'd been keeping it at the back of the drawer we normally keep the batteries, the screwdriver we never use and a key we've been keeping for at least a decade, despite the fact we haven't got a clue what it unlocks.

One of the daily acts of kindness I've adopted, learned from my amazing cousin, is to tell the people I love that I love them at least once a day. Normally Cassie just nods, Charlotte rolls her eyes and Sophie says "I know, Dad" but when they don't think I'm looking I catch the smile, and they almost always respond with a 'I love you, too'.

The subject of love came up the first time I interviewed Bernadette and we chatted about how we should 'take back' Valentine's Day. Bernadette told me that, instead of Valentine's Day being the purely commercial affair it's turned into, she'd like to ensure that Valentine's Day is what it was originally designed to be.

For Bernadette the way we take back Valentine's Day isn't by words, it's by action. That's why kindness for Bernadette is a consistent habit involving taking practical action to make the world a kinder place. For Bernadette, kindness isn't theoretical; it's practical. It's about taking positive action each and every day. It's about making the world a better place one kind act at a time.

As a celebration of love.

HOW WOULD YOU DO THIS?

Telling the ones you love that you love them is a kindness. We all want to be wanted, we all want to be needed, and we all want to be loved. Try it today with the ones you love. I doubt very much you'll be disappointed with the result.

Smile

Over the past few years I've developed a strange habit. One that I've observed not many people do in public very often, particularly in London.

I started out doing it on public transport. I started slowly, realising that the worst that was going to happen was that I'd embarrass my family and might get a couple of funny looks, and then I started doing it more often.

I started doing it at home. In the office, while walking down the road, in the pub, on a plane. I started doing it when on my own. I started doing it with friends. I got really confident doing it, and some might say too confident doing it.

The strange thing about that when you do it to someone else they start to do it too and the odds are you'll both feel a little bit better for it.

So, what is this incredibly contagious and initially embarrassing, but ultimately fulfilling habit?

It's smiling. An act so simple, but so incredibly powerful.

However there are a few reasons I believe smiling is such a simple way to be kind. But first let's look at the benefits of the simple smile.

Smiling improves your health. Smiling releases cortisol and endorphins. These brain chemicals provide a bunch of health benefits including reduced blood pressure, increased endurance, reduced stress and a stronger immune system.

Smiling improves what others think about you, but strangely only in certain places in the world. Different cultures view smiling in different ways. If you're in Russia, South Korea, Iran, Japan, France or the Kerala region of India smiling is considered a sign of less intelligence. However, in the majority of the places in the world including the UK, China and the USA someone who smiles more is considered to be more intelligent, as well as being seen in most countries as more honest too.

So, not only does smiling make you feel better, and the recipient of the smile feel better, in most countries you'll be seen as smarter and more trustworthy. All for a simple movement in the lips and eyes.

There's one thing worth mentioning here - only smile at strangers if you feel comfortable!

One of the most insightful parts of my chat with Bernadette was when she was talking about people only performing acts of kindness they feel comfortable with. While, as a bit of an extrovert, I'm really relaxed about smiling at strangers, you might feel it's a bit strange.

Nobody believes that you should go around grinning like an absolute madman. However, it might be worth giving someone a quick grim on the tube, in the office or at the gym. In Bernadette's *Little Book of Kindness*, she suggests that you might want to turn it into a bit of a game, setting a target for the amount of times you smile in a day and then trying to beat it the following day.

This quick simple gift of smiling will make both of you feel slightly better, it doesn't cost you anything and is certainly worth giving a go next time you're out and about.

Smile: A Poem by Spike Milligan

Smiling is infectious,
you catch it like the flu,
When someone smiled at me today,
I started smiling too.
I passed around the corner
and someone saw my grin.
When he smiled I realized
I'd passed it on to him.
I thought about that smile,
then I realized its worth.
A single smile, just like mine
could travel round the earth.
So, if you feel a smile begin,
don't leave it undetected.
Let's start an epidemic quick,
and get the world infected!

Say thank you

We all like to be appreciated - but sometimes you've got to be the recipient of an act of kindness to understand its impact.

Once I had the privilege of helping a fellow financial planner when he was thinking of starting his business. Keith is a lovely bloke who, while having a decent amount of experience as a financial planner, wanted to start his own business and sent me an email to see if I'd share some time and some of the lessons I'd learned along the way.

Building a business can be tough. There are plenty of books, courses and online resources that guide you in the right direction, but often speaking to people who have had the experience, as well as some of the bumps and bruises which come with business ownership, is helpful if you're just starting out.

I tried to help Keith as much as I could and invited him to an event I ran designed for financial planning and advice business owners to share best practice. Keith came along, participated actively in the debate, and although having to leave slightly early to get back up to Edinburgh seemed to get a lot out of it as well as contributing massively.

At that point I didn't think much more about it, until a few weeks later I received an item in the post. It was a small greetings card. On the front with under the image of a gold embossed little green whale was the phrase 'Thanks a ton' and inside the card written in neat handwriting was the following words:-

> *Dear Chris,*
>
> *One lost man in London seeking to speak with those who might be kind enough to share their story and perhaps help him on his journey.*
>
> *I cannot thank you enough for your kindness in inviting me to your group and of course the emails and telephone conversations, when I'm sure you have 1001 better things to be doing. I'm massively grateful.*
>
> *I move forward with no idea as to what the future might look like but I push on with enthusiasm and determination, nonetheless. Regardless of what awaits I will always be grateful for all of your wisdom ... so thank*

you.

I loved receiving and reading the very eloquently written Thank you note and the fact that Keith had taken the time to write something so meaningful and personal. This simple act from Keith reminded me of something really important - I needed to say thank you more.

You see 'I love you' are three powerful words but it's probably best to only tell people you actually love. For me that's my family, my friends (and my Amazon delivery driver). However simply offering thanks is such a simple, but powerful, way of being kind and the more unique the thanks the better.

I love Keith's handwritten card, but you'll have your own uniquely personal way of saying thanks. It might be a unique gift that shows the person you're thanking you really know them. It might be a smile and a hug for the right person. It might simply be the words delivered honestly and earnestly.

In all our workplaces, in our homes, in our social circles and in our daily lives we all have the opportunity to say 'Thanks' more. To our clients and customers, to the people we love, to the people who serve us every day. And especially to the people who support us the most when we need it. Saying thank you is very effective way to deliver a message of kindness.

When was the last time you said thank you?

Share good news

One of the greatest things about hosting the podcast is the fact that we get the chance to share stories of people doing great stuff in the world. One of the reasons we love to do this is not only does the sharing of these stories improve our own mental health, it also helps the people who listen.

There's plenty of negative news in the world and by sharing good news, hopefully, we can redress the balance and share examples of why, generally speaking, most people are pretty awesome.

While we've got a lovely podcast to share the stories of good news we may have picked a little bit of an extreme medium to deliver these stories and I'm pretty sure you've got better things to do than start a podcast about people being kind to each other. And frankly we could do without the competition!

However there are a few ways you can share stories of good news more simply and straightforwardly than starting a podcast.

Firstly, fill your social media feeds with stories of positivity, both personal and more broadly.

A friend of mine, Dave Forsdyke, wanted a more efficient way to cope with the recent lockdown during the Coronavirus pandemic. He started sharing daily silver linings stories, which made him feel hopeful and thankful during a period which was tough for all of us. We also picked up on the stories and shared them on the live episodes of the podcast and spread these stories a bit further.

All Dave needed to share these stories every single day was his Facebook account and a few minutes a day to do a little bit of research. The reality is that sharing anything today is easy. All it takes is an internet connection and an intention to do some good to share some kindness.

I believe we've all got a choice. We can use our social media platforms to moan, or share pictures of our travels, or loved ones, or funny pets (and who doesn't like a funny pet). We can comment on other people's photos and videos and

59

comments. We can join and build communities and contribute to them.

We can do all that - and, in addition to all of this, we can do something kind. We can share stories of kindness and positivity.

Be a helping hand

Have you ever had an experience where you've bought a new jacket, you're wearing a new shirt or you're driving a new car and suddenly you realise you're seeing this particular coat, top or motor vehicle everywhere you look?

Psychologists call this the frequency illusion (or the Baader Meinhof phenomenon) and explains how, when you're focusing on a particular subject your brain starts to highlight examples of your specific object of focus in the world.

I certainly found this to be the case when I started to think more about kindness, as I was seeing a lot more opportunities to be kinder while going about my everyday life. Not big elaborate acts of kindness but ways I could simply offer a bit of a helping hand.

From mums struggling with a buggy and a particularly troublesome set of stairs at a tube station to the homeless guy who sits outside Superdrug near Fenchurch Street station, the people who I could provide a quick helping hand to now seemed to be more obvious.

In Bernadette's book she mentions a few extra ways you can offer a helping hand including holding a door open for someone, or offering someone your seat, or passing on a newspaper once you were done with reading it - look around you, the opportunities are endless.

This kindness happens more when you're more conscious

of the huge number of opportunities to lend a helping hand. I'm hopeful that this book will be part of the catalyst to support you in doing this and it's also worth setting yourself a challenge.

Next time you're out and about in the world take a tip from Bernadette and look for one way to make one person's life a little bit better today. Be conscious of it and keep an eye out for opportunities to do this. If you share my experience, and as the Baader Meinhof phenomenon shows, you'll find a few more opportunities to help others by simply offering a helping hand.

Compliments matter

Now you're clearly smart, you're reading this book after all, so it's probably no surprise to you that paying someone a compliment is one of the simplest and most effective ways to perform an act of everyday kindness.

A genuine, heartfelt, specific compliment is one of the most powerful and simple ways to be kind and have the ability to make someone momentarily happy and give someone the strength to change someone's lives.

When I look back at my life there's plenty of examples where a compliment I've received has encouraged me to work harder, dream bigger or care more. Knowing someone else thinks you're worthwhile is a massively powerful force and I think we underestimate the power of a good compliment.

Think about the compliments you remember the most. Maybe it was from a teacher or tutor. Maybe it was from a parent or grandparent, aunt or uncle. Maybe it was from a colleague or friend. We know the power of compliments from the ones we receive and the impact it has on our lives

61

and how it made us feel.

We asked our podcast listeners what the favourite compliments they'd received were and their particular favourites were both simple and powerful.

From the deeply touching like…

"You're the best the human race has to offer."

"I know your mum would be so proud of the man you are."

As well as compliments I don't know I'd be that flattered to receive to be frank:

"You won't get far with your looks alone, but thankfully you get 10 out of 10 for humour and personality."

Compliments were remembered - mostly fondly, even the ones that contain an element of humorous backhand, and I would love to be someone who was known as the person who might have been responsible for encouraging, inspiring or supporting someone else so they remembered the compliment for decades.

That's not to say that every compliment will be remembered for decades. Some might just make someone momentarily happy, but even if that's the case showing your support is still worth it, right?

Kindness is often about being treated how we'd want to be treated and if you enjoy receiving a compliment, and who doesn't, why not be more intentional in giving out a compliment or two?

Be Curious and Listen

Since thinking and talking about kindness for a few years there's one skill I'm still learning to get better at - **listening**.

Not just listening while waiting for your turn to speak in a conversation. Not just asking questions so you can eventually provide the answer. Proper listening, with a desire to understand more.

One thing I've certainly understood more since starting to host the podcast is the desire for people to tell their story. Not only have our guests wanted to share the amazing work they're doing we desired in the early days of the podcast we wanted to hear the stories of our listeners and our friends on social media too.

That's why on every podcast we ask a question.

These questions range from the philosophical (like 'Are most people generally good?') to the trivial ('What's your favourite viral video?') all the way to the deeply personal ('What one thing do people assume about you that isn't true?').

Strangely some of the silly questions we ask tend to get people really excited with 'What's your favourite Muppet?' and 'What's your favourite biscuit?' although we all know that there's only one answer to the former (and if you don't say Animal you're clearly mistaken) and while there's a range of alternatives to answer the latter, the humble Jaffa Cake is disqualified due to the fact that it's actually a cake. The clue's in the name.

The reality is that while we want to be appreciated, approved of, liked, loved and cared for, there's also one thing we have a deep psychological need to be - and that's understood.

It's why listening deeply and asking people about their lives, loves and showing an interest in what they're about as people is an amazing act of kindness.

I'm lucky. I get to build relationships and friendships with my clients. I want to truly understand what they're aiming to achieve with not only their money, but also with their lives and help them try to achieve this.

However learning to listen and to be curious in the right way is also something I'm working to be better at too. I think for most of us we could potentially get better at listening and I'm certainly no exception.

Like many things you can do to become kinder it doesn't happen overnight. The intention to improve is important and while Oscar Wilde was certainly correct that 'the smallest act of kindness is worth more than the grandest intention' on a number of occasions the act of kindness does come from the desire and intention to be better.

If you want to be a little bit kinder, make a promise to yourself that you're going to listen better. Be genuinely interested in the answer. Ask more questions. Give people the time to provide you with a thoughtful answer. Listen like you're not just waiting to respond. Learn to become a better listener and then try to get better every day.

One of the simplest everyday things we could do to all become a little kinder is to become better listeners and while simple doesn't mean easy, it's something you can do to ensure that you can become better at being kinder every day.

Ask for help

Benjamin Franklin was an interesting chap. Not only was he one of the founding fathers of the United States of America, he was also an inventor, scientist, diplomat and civic activist.

One of his most scientific experiments involved him, deciding to pop out during a particularly aggressive storm with a kite, a key, a jar and a bit of wire to demonstrate the connection between electricity and lightening. A connection which, at this point in history, hadn't been fully clarified.

I'm not convinced that you'd catch me wandering around in a thunderstorm trying to prove any scientific theory apart from the fact that the intensity of the rain tends to increase the desire for any individual caught in said storm to want to find shelter at an increased velocity. The reality is that Ben Franklin was made of sterner stuff than I and going out in storms for the sake of science floated Ben's boat. I think we can cut him a bit of slack considering he was an undeniable polymath.

He was also known as a writer and philosopher, but one of the lesser-known facts about Benjamin Franklin is the fact that he was also an amateur, but clearly successful, social psychologist.

When Franklin served in the Pennsylvania Legislature in the 18th century, he wrote to a colleague, with whom he had an acrimonious rivalry, asking if he could borrow one of the colleague's most valuable books. It's important to note that Franklin and the man hadn't shared a kind word between them.

This man, despite not particularly liking dear old Ben at the time, obliged and lent him the book. Franklin read the book kept it for a week and sent it back promptly.

The next time the two of them met in the Pennsylvanian courthouse the man approached Ben in a really friendly way and following that the men became firm friends.

Upon retelling the story later in his autobiography Franklin told this story and described it in the following way:-

> *"He that has once done you a kindness will be more ready to do you another than he whom you yourself have obliged."*

Effectively Ben was saying if you want to build gentler, kinder relationships with your fellow man (or woman) don't be afraid to ask for a favour. Asking for a favour is a sign that you trust the individual you're asking enough to take the risk and as humans we are preconditioned to help, even if, using the example of Ben Franklin, we're not overly keen on the individual initially.

The other interesting factor here is what happens to us next. If we've helped someone it's difficult for us to continue to view that individual in a negative light. After all, why would you help someone you disliked?

It's interesting. We believe asking for help is a weakness, but the evidence says that it's a strength. It's a way to show the person you're asking you trust or respect or like them enough to put yourself out there. Asking for help is something we should all get a bit better at.

We should be asking for help when we need a lot more.

We should be asking for help in the workplace.

We should be asking for help at home.

We should ask for help from our friends and our family

We should ask for help from even people we might not know particularly well, if we want to build closer relationships.

If you want to build better, deeper, more connected, kinder relationships - ask for help. Be vulnerable and build deeper connections with those you like and people you'd like to know better, by simply asking for help.

The helper's high

While asking for help might be quite an unusual way to be kinder a more direct way is to say 'yes' to someone who asks for your help. Some would argue is that doing someone a favour, regardless of whether you've been asked or you've offered, is the purest act of everyday kindness you can provide.

One of the most interesting elements of performing kindness, even a very small favour, is the physiological reaction we get when we help someone else.

When we do someone a favour or perform any act of kindness, our brain produces chemicals called endorphins. Endorphins work in our bodies to reduce pain and increase happiness and have the ability to produce a feelings of euphoria.

There's a bunch of ways an individual can trigger the production of endorphins in their own bodies. It's been shown that vigorous exercise is one way, but if the idea of putting on your trainers and banging out a swift 10k doesn't sound like your ideal way to spend your time, there are other ways you can get a natural boost of these internally-produced wonder chemicals

Sex has been shown to increase endorphins. Eating chocolate is another. I suppose doing both at the same time generates double the endorphins, but to be frank I haven't tried that!

The phenomenon of becoming happier by helping others has even been given a specific name - Helpers High. Literally the natural high you get from doing someone a favour because endorphins are released. So when someone asks you a favour, if you're able to support them with time, effort and energy, while continuing to be kind to yourself, please say 'yes'. It might be a family member who needs your help, a lost tourist looking for directions or a friend who needs a listening ear.

Offer someone a helping hand when they need it, whether it's offering to make the drinks in the office, helping to carry a child's buggy down some stairs at the tube or train station, holding a door for someone or giving someone your parking space. Not only will you support someone else who needs your help, but you'll also benefit from the flood of endorphins which have been directly shown to make you happier. Keep an eye out for opportunities to help and you'll find them everywhere.

...and if that isn't a win / win situation I don't know what is!

Anonymous daily acts of kindness and the art of adventure.

There are a few stories Bernadette tells in her amazing book, the *Little Book of Kindness* (available in all good bookshops online and in your high street) where she performs acts of kindness for people who she doesn't know and she will probably never meet again - just to brighten up their day a little bit.

One particular story was the time, on Valentine's Day 2012, she and a few of her friends delivered Valentine's cards to total strangers and, while the odd few were cautious, most people loved receiving this random gift from someone they didn't know.

Bernadette travelled all over London on that day and clearly from the way she writes about it had an amazing adventure.

The way Bernadette describes this story is as a fun escapade. She met a milkman, police officers and a man dressed as a mobile phone and Bernadette and her friends managed to put a smile on strangers. It made me think about ways I could deliver a bit of fun to strangers and have a bit of an adventure and it raises an interesting question.

What might you do to help a stranger today in a way where it feels like a fun adventure for you too?

However it's important to mention that 2012 wasn't a one off event but the start of something new that continues to this day. Every year, in an effort to reframe Valentine's day as a celebration of love and an opportunity to share some positivity, Bernadette hits the streets spreading the love across London and beyond.

You see, for Bernadette, this isn't a fad. It's a way of life. It's those consistently kind actions which, for Bernadette, makes the world a better place. For this desire to make the world a better place and a clear understanding that it takes practical action, I've got a lot of love for Bernadette.

In conclusion

Hopefully, in this chapter I've outlined just a handful of ways you can perform daily acts of kindness. Kindness that won't take too much time, but can be incorporated into your day-to-day life.

In the next chapter I'll be exploring Kindness that costs a bit more - not in pound notes, but in valuable time.

Chapter 3
The gift of time

The value of time

On an early Saturday afternoon in mid-November 2019 I was sitting staring at my laptop. While it's rare I work over the weekend on this particular occasion I found myself a bit bogged down with work I had to complete.

I was putting the finishing touches to a specific piece of client work that when I looked to my right and saw Sophie, my eight year old daughter, loitering around the sofa where I sat. This was unusual for Sophie as she wasn't known for her loitering.

Sophie usually - and how do I explain this politely - has a bit more of a direct communication style. She's more likely to just tell you what she wants or, on occasion, order it, as opposed to ask.

However today she was in a more diplomatic mood. "Daddy," she started, "Can I ask you a question?"

"Not right now Soph," I replied, "I'm working"

"But Dad, I need your he…"

"NOT NOW!" I interrupted, slightly annoyed, "I need to finish…"

"But I need your help with something."

It was clear at this point I wasn't going to complete this piece of work without first at least understanding what

Sophie wanted me to do.

"OK," I said closing my laptop case and setting the computer to one side. "What can I help you with?"

She held out her hand out to take mine. Again an unusual thing for Sophie to do as she's more likely to point the same hand towards where in the general direction she wanted me to be located.

I took Sophie's hand as she led me to her playroom, which is situated at the other side of the family room - our lounge and dining room area, as well as every now and again when I fall asleep in front of the telly, a bedroom!

In the middle of her playroom area sat a large box. As I remember it was the result of a particularly bumpy Amazon order.

"This…" Sophie announced proudly, "Is Dexter's new bed!"

Dexter, the family dog, already had a perfectly good bed - soft, cosy and warm. I wasn't convinced this box was going to be any better, but convincing Sophie was going to be a different proposition.

"OK," I said, "So what do you need some help with?"

"We need to colour it in," Sophie said felt tip pens at the ready…

I looked back at the sofa and the laptop. "I can't I'm afraid, Sophie - I need to finish a piece of work."

While Sophie looked a little disappointed she didn't make a fuss.

I walked back to the laptop, opened it and carried on working on behalf of this client. In the corner of my eye I could see Sophie colouring the box alone. She was happy doing this independently, but something inside me told me that I'd made the wrong decision.

A few years before I remember having a chat with a friend of mine about his dad. His dad was an accountant who was massively obsessed with financial security and success. His dad worked incredibly hard and built considerable wealth, but at the expense of having a close relationship with his kids.

When my friend thought about the memories of his dad there were a few in later life, but few from when he was growing, up as his dad was 'always working'.

As my friend's children were growing up he decided not to be like his dad and make a genuine commitment to spend time with his kids.

It might be playing, it might be chatting, it might be doing nothing, but instead of time 'working' he'd vowed that the time he spent with his children would be worth whatever financial impact this had on his life. I reflected on this conversation and while people have to choose how to live their lives I agreed that I had to be more conscious of spending time with my girls as they grew up.

Doing it was not as easy. Often I've got it wrong and continue to do so. However on this particular occasion I was fortunate enough to remember the conversation with my friend and the promise I'd made to myself.

I put my laptop down, strolled to the playroom and sat down next to Sophie.

"Sophie," I said as I pointed to a part of the box "What colour should this section be?"

"Red," said Sophie with certainty. "Definitely red."

We spent an hour turning the box from a dull brown box

into - a dull brown box covered in quite a lot of felt tip pen. A new home that our particular canine had not a shred of interest in. However while we coloured we sang, we chatted and we laughed and I realised what Sophie wanted wasn't for us to paint a box for the dog. She wanted to play. She wanted my attention. She wanted something far more valuable.

She wanted *time*.

I'm with Greek philosopher Theophrastus, student of Plato and the man considered the father of Botany when he said…

> *"Time is the most valuable thing a man*
> *can spend"*

So, if you're aiming to donate some time to be kinder this chapter is definitely for you. I'm going to share some ideas on how you might use your time (but no money) to ensure you're supporting causes you believe in, helping those most in need and feeling good about it along the way.

My guide for this particular chapter is Mr Patrick Luong. Patrick is the best person I can think of to guide us through how you spend your time effectively to be as kind as possible.

Patrick's story is an interesting one. He used to be a financial planner helping people work out what their hopes, dreams and motivations were and found that despite being highly qualified and amazing at what he did, he didn't want to be a financial planner anymore.

Instead he wanted to spend more time giving back to his community and raising both awareness and funds for good causes. So by day Patrick can be found working for Glass Door, a London based homeless charity and in his spare time you can find him helping others by organising his local parkrun, or combining doing good and fitness by getting involved in the organisation GoodGym as well as much, much more.

So let's start to explore, along with Patrick's help, some of the most effective ways you can give your time to help others and spread a bit of kindness in the world.

Giving blood

As an atheist it's pretty rare nowadays that I find myself in Church. In fact, there are only a few events where I'll visit any sort of holy ground:

- Marriages
- Funerals

and

- When I give blood

It's interesting to see some people's reactions when I talk about giving blood. Most people are fine with it or do it themselves. Others recoil in horror.

"I can't do that Chris" they tell me and go on to explain that they're afraid of needles, or they don't have the time or they don't like the idea of someone taking just under a pint of their blood in one fell swoop!

However, if you're thinking about giving blood (and I'd suggest you do) here are some reasons why you might want to consider doing it:

Firstly, and I wanted to start with one of the most important reasons - **you get to be cheeky to nurses without actually visiting a hospital!** I don't know about you but there is something about nurses, male or female, which makes me want to start to crack (usually very bad) cheeky jokes.

Maybe it's that they are in a position of authority and my nervous reaction is to crack a joke. Maybe it's the fact that I'd do anything to avoid the implication that seeing a nurse usually means I'm sick. Maybe I've just seen one too many carry on films. I'm not sure but being cheeky to a nurse is certainly something I love!

Giving blood provides an opportunity for you to indulge in a bit of medical related cheekiness without actually being sick and that my friends is a win / win for sure!

Now we've established the most important reason let's talk about the second most important reason for giving blood - **there's free biscuits!**

Now I know we can all buy a pack of biscuits from the shop. However, we also know the best things in life are free and this principal especially applies when we're talking about biscuits (and, erm, possibly a banana milkshake). Also, you wouldn't go into the shop and buy an individual shortbread, then an individual digestive and then an individual Jacob's Club If you go to give blood you've got a smorgasbord of biscuit choices from the humble Hobnob through to the all-so-familiar custard cream. Although there are never any Jaffa cakes - probably because they're not really biscuits.

Now in reality we all know that these biscuits aren't free. It's like a good old-fashioned bartering system where you swap some of your blood for some biscuits.

But here's the genius bit - and the third reason I give blood -**the body just makes you more blood very quickly**. One of the amazing things about the human body is its amazing ability to replace the blood you've given. It only takes a day to replace the plasma and a few weeks to replace your red blood cells. Your body produces 2 million red blood cells a second so it doesn't take too long to get you back to standard levels.

They do recommend that men wait for 12 weeks before donating again (16 weeks for women), which means that buying biscuits from the shop might be a better move for that daily digestive craving, but the fact that your body can cope comfortably without the blood you donate and then it's quickly replaced means donating blood is a bit of a no brainer.

However there is another reason I give blood - **it allows me to directly give to the NHS**. One of the institutions that makes me proud to call myself British is the NHS.

It's not perfect, it can be bureaucratic and it's had its challenges, but often I think we take the NHS for granted. This becomes even clearer when you consider how healthcare is provided (or often like many not provided!) across the pond in the good 'ole USA

The NHS helped bring my two daughters into this world and have continuously looked after Sophie, Charlotte, Cassie and I whenever we've had concerns from health scares to premature births to eye scratches.

However, while a bit of the tax I pay undoubtedly goes to the NHS to fund its services, giving blood allows me to support a service I believe in directly. Which is why giving blood is so important to me.

There is also another reason - **giving blood saves lives**. That's my bottom line

Giving blood saves lives.

It's simple isn't it.

- **Giving blood saves lives**
- **Giving blood costs you nothing**
- **Giving blood means you get biscuits.**

To be frank I'm a bit surprised more people don't do it. If you've been thinking about it, but never taken the jump, take a look at www.blood.co.uk, which is packed with resources and information.

Oh, and if you do decide to give blood -keep your hands off the Hobnobs. They're mine!

So, as I venture into becoming a kinder person giving blood was going to be the logical first step; I just wasn't sure what I was going to do next…

Sharing time…and expertise

I remember the first time I walked into a secondary school the first time since I left mine at 16. It was an open day and I was being guided around by a young lad who was enthusiastically showing us the facilities of the school. This was so that Cassie and I could decide whether it was the right secondary school for Charlotte to join.

That venture back into a large secondary comprehensive school, especially compared to Charlotte's smaller junior and even smaller infant schools, was making me concerned. How would my daughter, who was eleven at the time, cope with the maze-like corridors, the hundreds of older and mostly bigger kids and the continuously-increasing workload secondary education brings?

Looking back I should have realised my concerns were groundless. Charlotte has always loved school and, despite the change of environment, the transition from junior to senior school was something she took in her stride.

I get to visit the school every now and again on open evenings and school concerts, but until the past couple of years that was the limit of my involvement with the school.

However, as part of my kindness project I've found myself recently visiting the school a bit more often for another reason. You see for one of my acts of kindness I wanted to do something to help children understand a little more about a subject which I believe needs a more focus.

Money

There's plenty of evidence to illustrate that, as a nation, we just don't do enough to support people to understand more about their financial affairs and the statistics make this clear.

According to the Office of National Statistics, our debts continue to rise with a 7% increase between 2012 and 2017. This means in recent years we've taken on more debt than ever before.

The amount we save as a nation continues to dwindle and slipped below 2% of household income for the first time in years. This means that, as well as building up significantly greater levels of debt, we're also saving a lot less for our future than ever before.

My favourite statistic on the subject comes from a 2015 survey from Nationwide; a decent number of people know the meaning of LOL (79% of people surveyed), but a lot less knew the meaning of the financial acronym APR (54% of people surveyed) - it stands for annual percentage rate. Over a third of Britons nod along in financial meetings although they don't understand some of the financial terminology being used.

Now you could argue there's a number of reasons why the statistics suggest we're less competent at managing our own finances than ever before, from a more consumerist culture to increasingly busy and complicated lifestyles.

However, the reality is that most of these issues can be resolved with more financially educated and informed adults and this journey starts with more educated and informed young adults. To generate educated and informed young adults you need to start educating younger children about money.

I believe that we need to help our young people understand not just the basics of money, but also the simple tips, tricks and techniques those who are more proficient with money use. Potentially this would change how financially successful our future generations become.

It may seem ironic that in a book about kindness I find myself talking about the importance of wealth and I want to explain my perspective.

I believe that being good at personal finance is an important skill to have. While money doesn't make us happy, it's certainly true that a lack of money can increase stress and worry. Also accumulating wealth allows us certain freedoms. Freedoms to try new things, have new experiences both now and (if we're saving as we should) in the future.

I also believe that we owe it to the future generations to help them develop good personal financial management skills and I'm certainly not alone. There are a number of fantastic organisations, like the Personal Finance Education Group, The Money Charity, Redstart and MyBnk, who are working with young people across the UK supporting their financial education.

According to recent MyBnk statistics in 2007 only one in ten of UK adults had ever received any financial education. The good news is that the number of individuals who have received financial education is increasing - thanks to the efforts of these organisations. However, there's still an incredible amount of work to do.

Back in October 2017 I was proud to be sitting in a meeting room in a local school. Alongside me were a couple of teachers and a couple of ex teachers who now work for the London Institute of Banking and Finance.

We were there to discuss the fact that I wanted to sponsor a classroom of young people to go through the financial education course that is run by the London Institute of Banking and Finance. The course is designed to be an introduction into a bunch of financial concepts and to encourage the students to think about some of the aspects of money management they'll need to consider as they enter the adult world.

So there I was in a room full of educators, three of whom were certainly younger than me.

"You know some of the habits you have at school never leave you," I said, "like when you're a forty year old man in a room full of teachers, and still don't know if I should call you 'miss'."

There was a laugh in the room, which I was grateful for.

"So, this is how I want to help," I started, "Firstly I want to act as a sponsor to ensure the kids can go through the course. Secondly I want to support you, time permitting, in delivering elements of the course. Thirdly I want to make sure we shout about the work we're doing here - I reckon more schools should be providing money education, more financial professionals should be sponsoring these schemes and more noise should be made about how important these projects are."

"That sounds all feasible," said Julie, the inspirational Head of Financial Capability at the London Institute of Banking and Finance, "and thank you."

"OK," said Jo, the teacher responsible for leading the project for the school. "Where do we go from here?"

We spent another half an hour talking through the details and agreed that the course would start in November with me coming in to support my first class in the first week of December.

However as the time got closer I became more nervous.

You see I don't know how much public speaking you've done, but for me it always starts in the same way. The heart beats a little bit faster. I stumble over the first couple of words and then after the words start to flow and the heart settles down as I start to enjoy the experience.

While I've done a decent amount of public speaking over the past few years I still get nervous every single time. The reality is that, despite having the opportunity to speak to rooms full of hundreds of adults in the past, a classroom full of teenagers was making me feel quite nervous!

"Daddy – it's a spider!" Sophie (my 6 year old) screamed as she jumped off the sofa and ran to the other side of the room...

I laughed. "One thing you've got to remember Soph," I said, "Is that those spiders are more scared of you than you are of them."

"OK," said Sophie now breathing more deeply "What shall I do?"

"You've just got to face your fears, pick up the spider and take it to the garden."

As we looked over to the spider, which then decided it was time to leave the sofa and scampered off towards the open door towards the garden.

"He probably heard us," said Sophie as she clambered back onto the sofa, happy that her arachnid friend had decided to find an alternative place to rest his legs.

I find myself thinking about this little amusing vignette from my life as I stand outside a classroom.

"Remember Chris," I say to myself, "They're probably more intimidated by you than you are by them."

I was just spending a little time talking to young people about money on a hot sunny Wednesday morning.

The reason?

Firstly young people would benefit from understanding more about basic financial concepts as well as some of the practicalities of the impact of money in their daily lives.

Secondly I believe in 'doing well' and 'doing good'. Running a profitable growing business is fine, but we need to do our best to make a positive impact in the world too.

Thirdly I quite like a challenge. I like trying new things which are a little out of my 'comfort zone.' And I was definitely out of my comfort zone. I'd presented plenty of times in the past sometimes to pretty large audiences, but audiences

The teacher, Jo, and I went into the classroom and waited for the pupils to arrive.

"I've got to tell you," said Jo, "They're a pretty quiet bunch!"

"OK," I said wondering if this might absolutely bomb with no audience engagement.

The young people came into the room, Jo introduced me and I started to speak.

I tried to ask loads of questions and I needn't have worried as the young people got involved and answered them.

We talked about the cost of living, risk and fraud and there was a wide range of answers to my questions on each subject.

A couple of the kids had questions of their own and, while it was - as predicted - a pretty quiet bunch, as I walked around the classroom when they did their individual work they chatted to me about what they were doing and asked me a bunch of additional questions. And in no time the lesson was over.

These were my thoughts about the experience.

Firstly I was surprised how knowledgeable some of the kids were.

One particular boy seemed to be uncannily accurate on what the average property prices both in 1977 and 2018! Others understood many different concepts, including how shares work, scams and diversification. The level of knowledge was both surprising and really encouraging.

Secondly the fact that schools are happy to engage with professionals who want to help.

Working to help schools wasn't something I'd considered before, but trying to help the school in a tiny way by sponsorship as well as my engagement was really useful, and really, really rewarding. I'd encourage other professionals to get involved!

And thirdly, I think I'll stick with running a financial planning business instead of teaching!

While the feeling of intimidation melted away pretty quickly when I started to chat to the kids, I've got a huge amount of admiration for teachers. I can see why teaching is so rewarding, but I think I'll stick with working with individuals and business owners and leave the teaching to the proper education professionals.

Thanks to the team at Sanders and the young people in the class we're sponsoring - we look forward to working with you both now and in the future!

The genius of GoodGym

In a world where time feels like it's at a premium the struggle might be to invest time in doing good, while sacrificing time with friends or family, or even losing the time we need to focus on our own physical fitness.

This is where the concept of 'GoodGym' is seriously genius. Effectively it allows you to spend time tripling up on three areas of our lives which are shown to benefit our own wellbeing.

GoodGym combines two elements vital to our own wellbeing smashing together both our physical wellbeing with what we contribute to our communities.

Effectively GoodGym is a running club, but like no other as it combines every run with supporting someone with a community project. This might be to run to the local community gardening project, help out at said project and then run back. Doing this means that you're keeping fit and positively contributing to the economy, as well as strengthening social connections with other runners.

GoodGym started in 2009 and now, with 58 areas in the UK from Barnet, Bath and Blexley all the way through to Woking, Worthing and Westminster, the number of groups are exploding all over the UK.

Similarly to the way Parkrun combines fitness and

community in a way that's welcoming, inclusive and friendly, GoodGym adds the element that clearly makes it both powerful and popular, the ability to give back.

Since GoodGym started its runners have completed 210,000+ good deeds with over 15,000 of these tasks designed to help community projects, nearly 30,000 visits to support the needs of an older person and everything else in between.

Patrick is a regular attendee of GoodGym runs and has done everything from fetching shopping for someone in need, through to helping make a local community garden look amazing and is a massive advocate of GoodGym.

When we interviewed Patrick for the podcast we talked a lot about GoodGym. Patrick told me he loved the combination of keeping fit in addition to doing a bit of good! We spoke about how he'd spent time actively supporting his local community. This, over the time Patrick has been involved with Good Gym, included painting buildings, litter picking, helping out at a homeless shelter and even getting involved in a dance class!

Whilst it sounds like the big community projects are something GoodGym are amazing at, the support they provide to their communities doesn't stop there. Patrick talked passionately about the fact that some of his favourite acts of good were helping out a particular elderly person with a really specific task.

This might be as seemingly simple as changing a light bulb, which might be simple for you or me, but can be a physical struggle for someone who is a little more frail. I often find when I talk about kindness it is the simple things and, in particular, the things we take for granted that are valued the most.

Patrick's support, as part of GoodGym, is helping people who need a lending hand for something small. He feels this is one of the fundamental parts of being part of this amazing community.

I haven't yet managed to get myself along to help GoodGym out yet, but I have signed up so that when it does come to my local area I'm ready to try the GoodGym experience directly.

Thankfully, according to the GoodGym website, the work you do when you help out a local elderly person or at a community project is 'low-skilled'. Considering my ability to magically turn one intended piece of flatpack furniture into something clearly not as practical - that's probably about my level! Never before has an IKEA bookshelf and desk been magically turned into a piece of sculpture so provocative that Damien Hirst would be proud of it - but with no practical use at all. It's the reason I don't get the asked to do anything practical in my house, my only responsibilities typically involve lifting, throwing and destroying (instead of making or creating), which, to be honest ,is something I'm completely at ease with.

One of my favourite books describes the factors which contribute towards our wellbeing. In a masterstroke of book naming the book is called *Wellbeing*. It's an incredibly insightful book by Dan Rath and Jim Harter.

These factors are financial wellbeing, social wellbeing, community wellbeing, physical wellbeing and career wellbeing.

The true genius of GoodGym is it allows you to combine at least three ways to improve your own wellbeing and, through the acts of good you do, improving the kindness of others, in an amazingly time efficient way. It's done with other people so it's an intensely social activity. It involves exercise so improves physical wellbeing and it's about helping others in your local area which improves your community wellbeing. That's why I love the idea of GoodGym and when it comes to my part of the world will get involved. I hope you do too.

The art of companionship - how to make new friends

If at any time of your life you've felt lonely, and I know I have, you're not the only one. In a recent survey by the campaign to end loneliness a massive 84% of people in the UK have felt lonely at some point in their lives, with a significant 13% feeling lonely all of the time.

The challenge with loneliness is that it carries a stigma. While we'd absolutely understand if someone else mentioned it, but that doesn't make it any easier to admit when we're lonely.

Recently I read an article by Mark Gaisford. Mark is a successful business owner in his early fifties who wrote about the fact that he had no friends.

I remember reading the article thinking how brave an admission Mark had made, but also thinking how Mark wasn't alone and how at times I'd felt lonely.

I've got an amazing family; I love my work and get to work with some amazing people and I've got a decent amount of freedom over how I choose to spend my time. One area of my life I've neglected in the past, though, is the time I spend either with existing or making new friends. This at times has resulted in me feeling lonely, not for any company, but for time spent with friends. I also think it's a bloke thing, and I reserve the right to be corrected, but in my experience fellas seem to be unable to put their hands up and admit loneliness and do something about it that becomes a self-fulfilling prophecy.

The research says that many of us experience loneliness, regardless of age, although the impact of loneliness increases as we get older. Over half of people aged 75 and over live alone and two fifths of all older people say that their TV is their main company. No wonder the impact of loneliness are devastating.

According to the research loneliness is likely to increase your risk of death by a staggering 29%. This is greater than the risk from being obese or smoking 15 cigarettes a day.

So, with loneliness being such an issue in our society today, what can we do about it - and how might we spend some of our time having a positive impact on someone else's life?

Jason Connon, a friendly Glaswegian dad of two who runs an insurance business and one of the loveliest guys I know, came on the podcast to talk about a scheme he's actively involved in, the Age UK befriending scheme, and he shared some really interesting insights.

For nearly six years Jason has been friends with a lady called Dellis, a lovely Liverpudlian who, at eighty, is twice Jason's age. Jason was paired with Dellis by Age UK as part of their process and during their regular chats they talk about a wide range of topics including politics, what's going on in the news and the thing they both love - the Beatles.

"It's interesting Chris" Jason told me during our interview "The relationship started off with me wanting to help someone feeling lonely and that's the reason I got involved.

"But now I'm just phoning my friend."

I love that. Just two friends, four decades apart, but close all the same, phoning each other for a regular chat. Both helping each other maintain a social connection to balance the loneliness we all can feel, and both feel good along the way.

I'd say that's a pretty decent way to spend time. It's kindness that becomes more - it's not something you feel you should do, but something you want to do.

Be my Eyes

When I was first starting to explore the subject of kindness I came across an app with an idea so simple, but so powerful that I know I had to speak to the creator to explain a bit more.

Be my Eyes is an amazing little app that connects blind and partially-sighted people with volunteers to borrow a bit of visual help over a live video call.

It's a simple idea isn't it? Connect someone who needs visual help with someone who can provide that help through the device the majority of us carry in our pockets every day and the concept has proven popular.

The founder is Hans Jørgen Wiberg and the photo that illustrates the apps launch isn't of crowds of people at some elaborate event Silicon Valley style. It's just Hans holding his phone while halfway through upholstering a chair and it might be the most Scandinavian thing I've ever seen.

It makes more sense when you realise that Hans is also a Danish furniture craftsman and clearly an expert multitasker as launching an app that will positively impact the world so much, as well as finishing a piece of furniture while you do it, is no mean feat.

The launch was clearly a successful one as there were more than 10,000 downloads on the first day although I do wonder if Hans ever actually finished that chair?

Since it launched, and at time of writing, the app has grown and grown in popularity with over 5.7 million volunteers speaking 185 different languages supporting over 400.000 blind or partially-sighted people across the globe.

When I spoke to Hans (back in 2017) for the podcast we talked about how *Be my Eyes* morphed from an idea into a piece of technology that had a practical application.

The idea for the App started when Hans was working as a consultant for the Danish Association for the Blind. Part of Hans' job was to talk to his clients about how to use new devices in their homes.

Hans knew through his lived experience and the work he did with his clients that every now and again it was useful to be able to – effectively - borrow a pair of eyes for just a moment. He understood the need for a little bit of help, for example, to read an important letter, pick the right shirt, or work out which of the cans in his cupboard was beans and not dog food,

He also understood that with the development of smartphone technology it was possible for blind or partially-sighted people to get help and the support they needed delivered straight through their phone.

However, whilst the smartphone technology did allow blind and partially-sighted people to get the help they needed from family and friends it also presented a problem. Let's say for example when you needed your help your family and friends weren't available or you felt uncomfortable continuously asking the same people for help.

Hans had an idea - why not build a platform to connect blind and partially-sighted people with volunteers who are happy to help? Volunteers who were happy to be the eyes of a blind or partially-sighted person to help them with a specific task.

However, Hans had a problem. Hans was a furniture maker not a coder and, whilst he could rustle up a mean table and chairs his skills didn't stretch to coding a global technology platform. That's when Hans had a stroke of luck…

You see one day Hans was listening to the radio and a university in Denmark was running an event called the *Start-up Weekend*. Hans saw this as the perfect opportunity to go and pitch his idea and see if he could get the help he needed to make his dream a reality.

Entry to the event was fifty quid - but Hans saw this as a win because part of the ticket price included free beer all weekend, so really Hans couldn't lose! Either he'd get his idea closer to becoming a reality. or he'd make the most of the hospitality on offer!

In the end though, he didn't have the opportunity to drink much beer. A number of people at the event loved Hans's idea and wanted to help. Hans started to build a team, and then moved onto raise some money. Then in November 2014 he officially launched *Be My Eyes* on the Danish App Store and, since then, *Be My Eyes* has gone from strength to strength.

Downloading *Be my Eyes* is free for both recipients and volunteers of the service, so it's certainly worth, excuse the particularly poor pun, taking a look and downloading *Be My Eyes* today.

In addition to spending your time running and helping, or befriending, or by being someone's eyes, or using your skills and knowledge to help the future generation there are loads of different ways you can help others with a donation of time, and there are loads of places to find something you might want to do.

You certainly won't be alone. It's estimated that nearly twenty million people every year volunteer in some form or another.

There are plenty of places where you can find out how to spend some of your time to help someone else out, but if you're in the UK I'd suggest you start by simply putting 'I want to volunteer' into Google to open up a wealth of opportunities to donate your time for the good of others.

However there's also new ways of giving your time for good popping up all of the time using technology as the driver.

Don Diffang has been one of my favourite guests on the podcasts. He came in to speak to Charlotte and I with a massive smile on his face, and an infectious enthusiasm which permeated our interview.

Don's story is an inspiring one, but in an unusual way. Don has a successful career as a scientist, but wanted to do something to ensure he was doing something positive to make the world a more collaborative place to be instead of a more polarised one.

So after a decent amount of hard work Don launched *Do Me A Favour Buddy* (DMAFB for short)which is a hub for people who want to ask for a favour or want to offer a favour to someone else.

The website, like the Facebook of Kindness, is a place where people swap favours. From people offering to teach coding or to help you learn to ride a bike all the way through to an offer of help that starts 'I'm no counsellor - but if you need me I'm listen' just scrolling through DMAFB is enough to restore your faith in humanity.

However, you can do much more than that - you can

actively get involved! Take a look at www.DMAFB.ME to start.

In conclusion

We've barely scratched the surface of ways you can donate your time to good causes, but all the things in this chapter provide potential places to start.

However, one place to donate your time and money is by supporting one of the amazing charities out there and in the next chapter I'm going to share many of the ways you can do this.

Chapter 4
When kindness is charitable

I've done some frankly ridiculous things in the name of raising money for charity. I've run, walked and jumped out of planes. I've abseiled from the top of large buildings although the way I abseiled would probably be better described as slowly falling.

I will very quickly skip over my other embarrassing abseiling story (the one where I spend twenty minutes bouncing off the 23rd tallest building in London) as I want to introduce you to my brightly coloured friend.

The first time I met Andy Furneaux he came striding into my office dressed head to toe in bright orange. He's carrying an orange bag, wearing a couple of orange badges and, just in case you felt he isn't orangey enough, is wearing a bright orange lanyard.

I don't know whether bright orange is an on-trend fashion choice, but it certainly suits Andy.

Andy is one of the most positive, inspirational people I know. He's one of these people who is immediately likeable, unfailingly friendly with an openness and honesty as he shares not only what drives him and how we loves the work he does, but also the fact that his life hasn't been without challenge.

Andy's in his early fifties, a big West Ham fan, a soul DJ and a loving dad. He's also a community fundraiser for Saint Francis Hospice, which helps care for people in East London and Essex, usually at the end of their life.

The reason Andy had come to my office on a cloudy Tuesday afternoon was to tell me about the amazing work of the hospice for the benefit of our podcast listeners and to - unintentionally - brighten up our office, which contains quite a lot of white and purple and clearly not enough carrot.

Now these was a reason Andy was wearing so much orange, it is the brand colour of Saint Francis, an organisation which cares for hundreds of people every year in the nineteen beds the hospice in itself and looks after thousands more in their homes.

The hospice employs 240 people, Andy being one, but this number is dwarfed by the fact that it also relies on the time, effort and energy of 870 volunteers who support the work the charity does. It's one of the largest hospices in the UK.

Throughout my chat with Andy you could tell that what Andy does for Saint Francis wasn't a job, it was a vocation. Something he believed in.

Andy started telling me that way before he was employed by the hospice he was a firm supporter. This started after his friend's mum became sick in her early fifties and the hospice really supported his friend and their family through such a difficult time.

Eight years ago Andy decided that he wanted to do something to support the hospice. So he set up an event to raise funds and also provide him an opportunity to spin some of his favourite tracks.

Then he received some bad news. While arranging this event he was told he was being made redundant, but decided that he'd continue with the fundraising for the hospice.

The event was a success and it also turned out that the

hospice was building a team of salaried fundraisers and asked Andy if he would join this team. With an opportunity for a new career in professional fundraising for a cause he firmly believes in, it was too good to pass up. Eight years on he tells me he hasn't looked back. However you can tell that Andy would do this for nothing. This isn't a job for him, it's a vocation.

Andy went on to tell me the massive amount of support hospices need to continue to provide the amazing support they give to families. For Saint Francis they need to raise £22,000 every single day. This couldn't be achieved without the network of shops, the amazing people who fundraise and the team at Saint Francis, of which Andy is a proud member.

When Andy left I spent a couple of minutes reflecting on the only personal experience I've had with a hospice. My grandad died in his mid-eighties and, just before his death, spent about a week in St Joseph's Hospice in Hackney, East London.

Knowing that it was likely it was the last time we'd see him, Cassie and I along with the then toddler Charlotte walked through the doors of the Hospice. I was nervous as I walked in, but remember being surprised at the sound of laughter when I was expecting a somber atmosphere.

My grandad had become pretty senile at this time, a shell of the strong proud man I'd once known, and told me a couple of times to break him out. The problem was, with my grandad, is I never knew whether he was joking or not, so he may have been serious or it may have been one last practical joke for old time's sake.

While we were there a nurse approached the bed and offered cups of tea, food for my grandad and juice for Charlotte.

Although we declined, the nurse said cheerfully, "If there's anything we can do to help," and I remember wondering how it was possible to be so positive while constantly surrounded by death. That was foolish of me in retrospect and I found myself wondering whether I still felt this way and concluded that I could now clearly see the positivity in helping someone be as comfortable as possible at the end of their lives.

I remember the confusion of some of the people at the end of their lives, but the patience, good humour and care the staff in the hospice, many of whom I'd imagine were volunteers, made the days before death as comfortable as possible and ensured that the families had good memories of the ones they loved at the end of their lives.

I remember Charlotte holding her tiny hands out and my grandad smiling. Charlotte smiled back as she lightly grabbed my grandad's fingers. I remember the simple pleasure of watching this and feeling grateful for this memory. I remember crying when we left the hospice knowing it was probably the last time I'd see my grandad, but grateful he was in a place where he'd be looked after.

I didn't see my grandad again. He died the day after our visit, but I knew I had a positive memory of him at the end of his life to go with all of the lovely memories I had of him from throughout his life.

Looking back, what I hadn't realised was how much work, time, effort, care and attention goes into providing this sort of care. Hospices care for tens of thousands of people at the end of their lives across the country, every year with both volunteers and paid professionals.

I also hadn't realised the ongoing cost of running a hospice. Saint Francis Hospice for example needs just under eight million pounds each and every year to continue helping people, not only in the grounds of the hospice, but also, and a lot of people don't realise this is a service many hospices provide, on the 2,500 home visits its staff performs each year.

The majority of the care for people like my grandad, or your mum, or your partners favourite aunt is in their own homes. People who crave dignity at the end of their lives and where hospices around the country, including Saint Francis, supports them to maintain their dignity when it's most important.

Raising money for your favourite charity can be done in loads of different ways. In this chapter I want to explore a couple of stories about why fundraising is so important. If I can inspire you to switch off your TV and go and do something less boring and more inspiring - and support a charity which means a lot to you I can say I've achieved something.

Run, walk and climb - do something physical for charity

Every year the London Marathon raises tens of millions of pounds for charity. Tens of thousands of people choose to run around the streets of our capital pounding the pavements for 26.2 miles.

If 26.2 miles feels like a long way to run - that's because it is. The first ever marathon was run by a Greek messenger over 2500 years ago. Having started at the coastal town of Marathon he ran the 25 miles to deliver a message to Athens confirming the battle, which was currently running in the town of Marathon.

However the poor messenger running in the Greek sun clearly wasn't prepared for the 25 mile journey on foot.

While he arrived at the capital to deliver the news and managed to articulate one word, "Victory", at which point he dropped down dead.

I've been on holiday to Marathon and during that time made a trip to Athens, although I took heed of the ancient courier's lesson and decided not to run. Instead. I caught a cab.

However, in modern times runners are a little more prepared to run this distance and they do it for 'fun'. They are sponsored for millions of pounds across the world to do so, which in turn raises the money that allow many charities to continue to run effectively.

In the UK, for a lot of charities, the London Marathon is the biggest fundraising event of the year and in 2019 over 66 million pounds was raised smashing through the figure for the previous year of just under 64 million.

However, it also meant another significant milestone. Since the launch of the London Marathon in 1981 the event has raised over 1 billion pounds in total. That's a lot of money to support the fine work by charities all over the UK.

I completed my first Marathon in 2017 in Paris. The experience was certainly a memorable one and included nearly getting attacked by a man with a baguette, possibly the most Parisian way to be accosted, and getting the call 15 miles from Cassie, Charlotte and Sophie to tell me that, not only a man wearing a giant tutu was at least four miles in front of me, there was also another gentleman who was quicker whose head was adorned with a giant Eiffel Tower.

Since then I've also managed to complete the London Marathon a couple of times and I was massively honoured to be able to raise money for a really amazing cause and supe- proud that this cause was Saint Francis Hospice.

Although my London marathon experience was a little strange to say the least.

You see I decided to participate in late 2019 and started to train ready for April 2020. As 2020 hit I started to get excited about the experience. so I spent the winter, including wet and rainy October, windy November and arctic December hitting the road.

By January I was getting into a bit of a decent routine and this continued until mid-March when I was going out and doing some really good longer runs!

Then the time came. When you're training for a marathon the recommendation is to do one decently long run before you actually go out and do the full distance. The 13th of March was the day I decided to see whether I could actually run a Marathon.

I'd had a busy day at work so upon returning home, and hit the streets. I ran 22 miles that day and felt mentally and physically ready to run a Marathon. Whilst it wasn't the full distance I knew if I could do 22 miles I could definitely complete the full run.

However, on returning home, legs tired and very hungry, I switched on my phone to find a WhatsApp message from a friend.

"Have you heard the news? The Marathon has been postponed!"

I really should have checked my messages before I went for that run!

At that point the run was rearranged for October, so I decided to continue my training and simply stay in Marathon condition. Not so easy in a particularly hot summer. It was tough to keep motivated when the news came in August that whilst the London Marathon 2020 was going to continue it wouldn't be the mass participation event everyone looks forward to.

Instead you could run the Virtual London Marathon, where you ran the 26.2 miles in a day, on your own, at your own pace, so to make sure I was still doing something that benefitted the charity I decided to do this.

On the 4th of October, whilst the elite runners were running laps of St James's park in a 'biosecure bubble' Cassie drove me to Chelsea Bridge, west of London where I ran down the banks of the river Thames all the way home.

The experience was a fun one. Plenty of people wanted to have the London experience without actively being involved in a mass participation event so on occasion I passed a few virtual Marathon runners and participated in what many runners do - a polite nod and smile, while running past.

The experience however became a little less fun on the last 6 miles. With no crowds as I ran through East London and the rain starting to come down, my legs feeling every single step of the preceding 20 miles and my Marathon running playlist running out of songs I was feeling a little less motivated. However I did make it to my front door. Now I thought I'd planned my route perfectly. The reality was that when I turned into my road I checked the app which told me how long I had to run.

Instead of telling me that I had the 200 odd Meters I assumed I'd have less, the screen gave me some disturbing news; '1.2 miles remaining'!

So, whilst I expected to be at home in the next couple of minutes with a nice cup of tea and looking forward to the longest powernap of my life, I had to stop running down my road, turn around and run a few laps around the block before finishing!

It definitely confused my family who were waiting at the door for my return only to see me start to run up to them, check my phone and then turn around and run away! But we got there in the end.

The 2021 London Marathon was a different experience altogether and a day I think I'll remember for a long time. The crowds were amazing, people were super supportive and generous and the experience, whilst physically challenging, was one I'm so glad I got involved in.

One thing I realised on the day of the Marathon that I didn't understand when taking on the virtual challenge - you are not alone. There are tens of thousands of people like you. Tens of thousands of people who are going through the same emotions. The excitement that the day had finally arrived. The fear, despite most people taking the training really seriously, of feeling that we hadn't done enough to prepare. The desire and determination to make sure that, regardless of the fear, they didn't let either the charity they were supporting or the people who sponsored them down.

For every name on every coloured vest, every charity logo, every nervous smile there's a story. A story of why they'd choose to support their particular charity in a way which requires such a huge personal commitment. Tens of thousands of people each year all join in taking on the personal challenge while helping others. If you ever decide to run the Marathon you'll have your own story to join all the others, every single one being equally important.

It surprised me, when doing the research for this book, the amount the London Marathon consistently raises for incredible causes. The majority of runners hitting the streets are doing so for the same reason. To raise money for amazing charities they truly believe in. Typically, the

London Marathon raises 60 million for a wide range of charities, many of whom regard the London Marathon as their biggest fundraising opportunity of the year.

I'd recommend anyone run a marathon at least once. While it's a tough challenge the sense of personal achievement, the support you get from family, friends, the charity you run for and people on the route is amazing and the feeling of euphoria you get at the end is unforgettable.

Also, and this is purely a personal recommendation, have a gin and tonic waiting for you at the end of the run. While personally, it helped me get through the last couple of miles almost pulling me towards the finish line it also might have been the best G&T I've ever tasted!

When it comes to running, walking or climbing there are thousands of other ways to raise money, which don't involve running a marathon distance.

You can run virtually any distance to raise money for charity and certainly plenty of people participate in 3-mile runs (5km or the length of the average parkrun) to raise funds for their charity of choice, many in fancy dress.

It's estimated that 5 million Britons have run for charity in the past year. Meaning that regardless of your fitness level or the distance you're comfortable with, if you do decide to run to raise money for a cause you really believe in you'll join millions of others in being more physically active and helping charities continue to do amazing work.

The National Literacy Fund is a charity which empowers disadvantaged kids by providing resources they need to ensure they have the reading and writing skills many of us take for granted. They do an amazing 'Where's Wally' run every year. Typically, this involves hundreds of participants jogging through a London park dressed as Wally. Charlotte and I have completed this particular run and it's an enjoyable Saturday morning out in London. Although it is a relatively easy run for the participants, it must be a confusing sight for many of the people visiting the park just to walk their dogs.

As cancer has had an impact on many of our lives at one stage or another, it's not surprising that many of the most popular mass participation running, walking and climbing events are for cancer charities.

- Cancer Research UK's Race for Life raises just a smidgen under 50 million pounds per year with the option to run either 5km or 10km.

- The Breast Cancer charity Walk the Walk encourages people to get involved in the MoonWalk, a stroll through London where people can choose to stroll either a half marathon or full marathon distance at their own pace and while in the company of their friends or fellow fundraisers. However, the moonwalk has one rule. Anyone walking must wear a bra, including the men.

For the more adventurous of us there's an opportunity to climb Kilimanjaro for charity, or walk the Inca trail or along the Great Wall of China. Doing a trek or challenge can tick something off your bucket list at the same time as raising money for a worthy cause.

The opportunities to run, walk and climb for charity are everywhere and are designed for all abilities. All it takes is a passion for the charity, a desire to do some good and a decent pair of trainers.

Jump and Swing - Do something daring for charity

To return to my abseiling experience, the first time I slowly fell down a large structure the structure in question was the Orbit in Stratford. Situated in the Olympic park the Orbit could probably be best described as part modern art, part viewing tower and part ridiculously elaborate Helter Skelter. At nearly 115 meters high it's the same height as 26 London buses stacked on top of each other.

On this particular descent I was raising money for Richard House, an East London based children's hospice and, while I'd been fortunate that our family had never needed the services, I knew Richard House provides an amazing service.

Leaning backwards off a large structure is never going to be the most natural thing to do, but that's how you start an abseil. You're meant to lean off and put your feet on a ledge just below the platform to start your journey downward. From this particular ledge you can adopt a relatively smooth descent. Instead I found myself one leg on the original platform and one leg aimlessly waving 377 feet about the ground in search of this ledge.

"I can't find the ledge!" I exclaimed to the expert abseiler at the top guiding us amateurs through the process of a successful abseil.

"Don't panic," he said. I started to panic. At which point I flopped down from the platform so I was now hanging in mid-air - and spinning.

"Don't worry!" the expert shouted down to me, "All you need to do is slowly let yourself down using the ropes."

I followed the expert's advice and slowly descended from the structure. However, my descent seemed to be different from the others I'd seen. Instead of a controlled descent in a relatively straight line I found myself in some bizarre pirouette turning all the way down to the bottom. If it had been intentional it could have been quite artistic - something not unlike a snippet from a Cirque de Soleil performance. Instead it looked like something out of a Norman Wisdom sketch.

I arrived on the ground and could see Cassie, Sophie and Charlotte at the bottom waiting for me. As I reached the ground and my ropes were removed I looked to my right and saw that Sam, the man who I'd been partnered with had also reached terra firma.

Sam, I'd found out while we were nervously chatting at the top of the Orbit, had a really important reason to get involved in raising money for Richard House. Sam's 9 year old son used the services of Richard House.

I thought about my girls. I tried to imagine how I'd feel if they suffered from a life limiting condition and had to use the services of a kids' hospice. I couldn't get past the terror that idea inspired in me. There was Sam waiting to throw himself off the tallest sculpture in the UK, a giant smile on his face despite having a child who was really unwell, ready to support a cause so important to him.

On that day my perspective shifted a bit. Donating or raising money for a charity can feel a bit impersonal. However, the reality is that the money you and I raise or donate goes to amazing causes designed to improve people's lives. People like Sam and his son.

That's why one of the kindest things you can do is to help fundraise for a cause you believe in. For people who really benefit people from it. Everybody knows a Sam. Sometimes Sam is a member of your family. Sometimes it's a neighbour or friend. However there are millions of us in the UK who have benefited from the amazing work UK charities do every day

If you ever want me to do something ask me when I've had a bit of booze, but you need to time it just right. Too sober and I'll probably say 'no', but too inebriated and that happens faster than it used to) I either won't remember or blame the booze for saying 'yes'.

Mr David Taylor is a fine gentleman who runs a charity - In Sue's Name - in memory of his daughter Sue, who died of a brain tumour back in 2011 at the relatively young age of 42. One fine evening David approached me at a business networking event.

The event involved about 150 people chatting about the organisations they ran and David explained that brain cancers kill more people under the age of 40 than any other cancer and yet less than 1% of the government's research budget goes toward research in this area.

David wanted to put this right and his target was over the next nine years was to raise one million pounds, every penny to go towards specialist research at the Brain Tumor Research Centre at Queen Mark University in Whitechapel.

David approached me with a smile on his face and a glint in his eye. After telling me a bit about the amazing work the charity was doing he asked me whether I'd be interested in, erm, jumping out of a plane to raise money for In Sue's Name.

Maybe it was the two bottles of beer I'd already consumed. Maybe it was the fact that David's charity was doing amazing work. Maybe it was the fact that David had set this charity up in memory of his daughter, which with two girls of my own struck a chord. Or maybe it was the fact that jumping out of a plane had been on my bucket list for some time and I hadn't been brave enough, or found a good enough reason, to do it.

However, regardless of the reason I found myself saying yes. Then immediately regretting it and deciding to quietly approach David at the end of the event to tell him I wasn't sure. But before I had the chance to do this the organiser of the event, Ted, stood up to welcome everyone to the event.

Halfway through his presentation he mentioned the importance of networking and said

"Getting organisations together to see how the might help each other works. It's one of the reasons we run these events. Even though we've still got plenty of time left - Chris Daems has already volunteered to jump out of a plane for David Taylor's charity In Sue's Name"

All eyes turned to me and I nodded timidly, smiled and shuffled a little awkwardly. There was no getting out of it now and I resolved to enjoy the remainder of the event.

In the morning I had a moment. One of those moments when you realise that you've volunteered, VOLUNTEERED, to jump out of a plane at 12,000 feet. I came into the kitchen that morning and Cassie was making coffee.

"How was last night?" she asked and I didn't say a word, but clearly the look I gave her was enough. She looked me in the eye.

"What have you done now?"

A few months later I'm wearing a less than flattering bright blue jumpsuit and feeling nervous. To satiate these nerves I decide to have a chat to my new best friend, Jamie, who is going to give me a sky-bound piggy back as I throw myself out of a plane ten thousand feet up.

Jamie, despite only being in his early twenties, is a calming presence. He tells me he's already had years and years of experience in jumping out of planes initially attached to someone else, then on his own and then being the expert who guided rank amateurs like me who wanted to raise some cash for an amazing cause.

Suddenly, I find myself on board the plane surrounded by eleven other jumpers all attached to their skydiving experts. I'm feeling nervous and Jamie is reassuringly tapping my arm every now and again.

I didn't think of it at the time but each and every one of these individuals were raising money for a cause they believed in. I'm sure there'd be plenty of debate on what's the most illogical.

Some might say that running around London for 26 miles, whilst there is a perfectly functional tube and bus service and plenty of taxis available might be a little misguided.

Others might say that not only jumping out of an aeroplane thousands of feet in the air, but also getting in the plane in the first place might be a little ill considered.

However there were still plenty of people that day, and I'm assuming most days, making the choice to take the jump to raise money for causes they believe in…showing that even if it's not the most logical choice in the world many of us go to extremes not only to challenge ourselves but also to help causes we believe in.

Before I know it we're shuffling closer to the door of the plane, which is now wide open. Let's dwell on that for a minute.

A plane.

Flying 10,000 feet in the air.

With the door open…

An open door which seems to be getting closer and closer.

Clearly it's not the most natural occurrence in the world and at the point where we reach the door I wonder why I'm not at home with a nice cup of tea, eating chocolate digestives and watching a Netflix box set. However, before I wonder why two bottles of Peroni and a nice gentleman asking a favour might lead me to leaping out into space thousands of feet about planet earth I'm suddenly falling. The thousands of feet between the ground and me and Jamie is decreasing at a rate of knots.

It's hard to describe what freefall - the time between jumping out of a plane and the parachute being deployed - is like. For me, there was a feeling of freedom. Excitement, deep exhilaration, but unexpectedly and, maybe counter-intuitively, not fear. It felt like the hardest part of a skydive had already been achieved, the element of actually exiting the semblance pf safety on board the aircraft.

Jamie pulled a lever and suddenly the parachute was up and we were floating downwards at a slower pace. I was given temporary control of the parachute in the form of two handles that allowed me to manoeuvre the parachute, but frankly I could have done without them. What I want when I'm floating thousands of feet in the sky is an expert to guide me down gently. I've been on plenty of flights in my time and never has the pilot called me into the cockpit so I could 'have a go'.

I did take temporary control, but my tentative approach aimed at a gentle descent clearly wasn't exciting enough for Jamie, who pulled one of the parachute controls and we became involved in a controlled spin,

As the ground approached Jamie took control and reminded me to bring my legs up at the right time and we both hit the ground bum first and slid along the grass.

"How was that?" Jamie said and at first I didn't know how to answer. If I had been more articulate at the time I would have said I was feeling a nuanced combination of fear, excitement, exhilaration, achievement and pride that I'd managed to raise a bit of money for an amazing cause. This all got consolidated into one word.

"Amazing," I told him, "Absolutely amazing!"

I absolutely appreciate that doing something you might not be entirely comfortable with for charity is at the bottom of many of our bucket lists. However, I'd humbly suggest that the next time you're considering a bit of fundraising it's probably worth doing something which scares you just a little bit.

When I got myself to my feet I was ushered onto a truck right next to the guy who had jumped out of the plane before me. As we chatted I asked him about his cause and he told me the amazing work he was doing at the Ministry of Stories, a writing centre in East London designed to help young people discover their confidence and potential through the power of writing.

That guy was Ben Payne and turned out to be an amazing guest, star of Episode 87 and 88 of *The Kindness Project* podcast. It's also definitely the strangest way I've recruited someone to come on and speak about their amazing work - after we'd both jumped out of a plane!

Maybe you won't skydive, or abseil, or mud run glamorously, but if you find something you can do, you will have a lot of fun doing it and raise cash for a good cause at the same time! What's not to enjoy?

Knit, slim or dress up - do something unusual for charity

One of the loveliest guests we've interviewed on *The Kindness Project* is a lady called Danielle Lazenby. Danielle came to my attention when I picked up our local paper and read her story, but the real thing that caught my attention was the picture that accompanied the article. It was of Danielle, who is in her early forties, surrounded by Christmas presents and dressed as a giant elf!

I've never been particularly good at pulling off fancy dress. I once went to a fancy dress party as Magnum PI, but found myself after losing the moustache twenty minutes into the night and spending the rest of the evening trying to explain why I was dressed as a man who had decided to wear a particularly gaudy Hawaiian shirt. However, it was clear Danielle suited fancy dress far better than I and was doing it for an amazing cause.

Danielle wasn't dressed as an elf just for fun - she was doing it to raise money for an amazing CAUSE.

Danielle has an obsession with Christmas. She loves Christmas so much, and she genuinely said this in our interview, her eyes dilate when she walks into the Christmas shop. She loves Christmas so much, if she had the choice, she would keep her tree up all year round. She loves Christmas so much that she decided to see if it was possible to actually become Santa - and that's where Danielle's story of kindness begins.

I love Danielle's sense of fun and enthusiasm. It's been amazing to see what she's done and get to know her and certainly she's one of the people you meet who, when she sets her mind to something, you know she's going to achieve it. However, even Danielle had to admit that becoming Santa was probably too much of a leap.

But Danielle hadn't given up on the idea, she simply needed a practical alternative. Chatting with her daughter about this idea one day she decided to explore how many children's hospices there were in the UK. A quick Google search revealed the answer was 54.

Danielle clearly felt this was achievable and set herself the challenge of visiting each and every hospice in the UK with presents for the kids. Next came the practical planning. Fundraising, mapping out her route and all of the stuff you need to work out for a jaunt around the country dressed as an elf!

Danielle got a bunch of people involved in the challenge including her mum who wasn't particularly impressed that she'd got the job of wrapping up all of the 1800+ presents that were going to be delivered to the hospice - particularly because the job included writing 1800+ gift tags to go with it.

Danielle started by delivering to some of the more local hospices at the start of December 2019, but then decided to go on an epic trip from the 20th of December until Christmas Eve travelling to Manchester, Wales and Liverpool to deliver presents directly.

Whilst Danielle didn't manage to physically get to every single hospice on her trip, she did send presents to the ones she didn't visit and plans to visit some of the ones she missed on the way. However, she did manage to physically visit 26 hospices and see the joy it created in the children's lives.

Speaking to Danielle about her journey, she told me that there were moments of pure joy – seeing the looks on some of the kids' faces as she delivered presents and the look on the faces of a number of petrol station employees as she casually strolled in to pay for her fuel dressed as an elf! She also shared some of the stories of knowing that she was delivering presents to children with only a little time left.

One particular story Danielle told me of a little girl in a wheelchair. The girl asked Danielle if she actually worked for Santa and Danielle told her she did. The girl then told Danielle that her mum and dad had arranged for her to have her Christmas early as she'd be an angel before Christmas Day.

Danielle did everything she could to hold it together and, in an act which shows how kind Daneille actually is, said, "I tell you what, when I go back to Santa I'll make sure he gets you an amazing pair of wings with glitter and lights"

The girl smiled and became really excited and the girls mum simply mouthed 'Thank you' to Danielle. The hospice let Danielle know that the girl passed away on the 23rd of December so never made it to Christmas, but I love the fact that in that particular moment Danielle gave that girl hope, something to smile about and, hopefully, by showing a little bit of kindness something for her family to remember.

Danielle is a shining example of one of the reasons I love interviewing people doing amazing things in the world. From the seed of an idea to the actual practical action you need to take to achieve anything. Some people might have called Danielle's idea ridiculous, but I think they'd be missing the point. The reality is that cynicism doesn't achieve anything.

It takes people like Danielle who are prepared to do something fun, go on an adventure and live their lives to help others who make a difference. If you're reading this I suspect you're one of these people too.

People are very inventive about their fundraising efforts. There are people who knit blankets and socks, people who walk their dogs, people who get sponsored for every pound or kilogram they lose. The wackier the better!

If you've got a hobby that you could get sponsorship for, it means you have fun while raising money - definitely a win-win. Be creative, be innovative - but do something. You'll get more than fun from your efforts - there's nothing like the warm glow you get from helping others.

Fundraising in the new normal

It's difficult to underestimate the impact the Coronavirus epidemic has had on charities.

According to research from the Institute of fundraising, charities were expecting their incomes drop by more than a quarter in 2020 due to so many live events being cancelled and the fact that these events are a massive source of funds for so many charitable organisations.

This impacts the majority of charities with 84% of charities seeing a decrease in income. There's an expectation that this reduction in expected income will continue - that's a lot of really decent charitable work not being done due to the impact of the pandemic.

Now we can hope that, as the virus takes more of a backseat, life will slowly become easier for these charities again. Hopefully, by the time you read this we'll be able to attend mass participation events again, so charities and the events that drive their income, are back on the calendar.

However, the other interesting thing to happen is how charities have evolved and continue to fundraise in the 'new normal'.

It seems that Zoom quizzing hit a new level of popularity during lockdown. Clearly this hasn't gone unnoticed in the charity sector as many more charities use online quizzing events as an opportunity to raise money for an amazing cause.

As everyone gets used to the 'new normal' and, as individuals, as businesses and as a society we've had to evolve, charities have had to do the same.

It's clear the COVID and the implications of COVID had an impact on charity donations.

With social distancing, lockdowns and most of us trying our best to support each other, getting together in large groups was not on anyone's agenda.

Recent research from the charity commission showed that 90% of charities experienced some negative impact from COVID 19 with 60% losing income.

It also meant that in 2020/21 97 charities were insolvent and this was 30% higher than in 2020. However, considering that there are 170,000 charities registered with the charity commission, it could have been a lot worse.

What this shows is that charities had to, and did, adapt to these changing conditions. Charities have proven themselves to be hugely adaptable with many changing their services and many medium-sized and large charities dipping into the reserves they hold for a rainy day to continue the support they provide.

The reality is that all charities benefit massively from 'live' events – and the pandemic meant that this type of fundraising venture was banned! However charities had to adapt and there were plenty of ideas which allowed charities to keep on raising money at a time when arguably many people needed as much help as ever…

Virtual charities quizzes were everywhere. People were donating the money they'd normally spend on their morning commute to charitable causes. Many of us were channelling our internal Paul Hollywood and raising money by baking – and, although I loved a bit of freshly baked bread, during lockdown I don't know whether my waistline could have taken much more by the end!

However, what these examples show is that charities have the ability to adapt and survive in tough times and time will tell whether, as we move back to a sense of normality, charities will benefit from the adaptations they've made during lockdown.

Regardless of what you think the future looks like, what it does show is there are plenty of ways to support the charities who do fantastic work at a time when their efforts are required the most.

I'm so glad that so many amazing charities exist. I read some research recently from the Charities Aid Commission that in our lives 98% of UK households will use a charities service at some point.

This might include visiting a charity-run museum or art gallery, getting advice from a charity or useful information from a charity website or directly using their services to help and support people when they need it the most.

One important thing to consider when thinking about charity is that, while clearly charitable organisations need cold hard cash to continue to help people, there are other ways you might be able to help.

It's not all about the money - giving the gift of - pens!

On a cold sunny autumn day at the start of November 2017 I found myself having a insightful chat in the pub.

In retrospect, a few too many of my most insightful conversations either start, stop or continue in the pub. I don't know whether I should be pleased, excited or surprised by that fact, but let me share the outcome of that conversation and what happened subsequently.

I was chatting with a fellow financial planner and business owner called Dominic and, while we had spent the afternoon in a coaching group talking about our respective businesses, the conversation had moved on to how I was trying to become more kind.

I explained that I'd found being intentionally more kind to people is a fantastically selfish thing to do and the fact that the science behind kindness seems to back this up.

There's always a danger in sharing this theory with people regardless of their profession, sex or creed. The eyes glaze over, a protective smile starts on their face and they slowly either start to check their phone (and often need to make an 'urgent call') or they just start to edge away from you.

However, on this occasion it was different. A broad smile spread over Dominic's face when I started talking about my kindness project and, as I explained what I was doing in helping out a number of kids with a start in financial education, he started to laugh.

"I completely understand where you're coming from," said Dom, "I try to help whenever I can and, while it's positive for the person I'm helping, I know that it'll make me feel great. I often don't understand why others don't get this."

"I know," I replied laughing too.

There we were, in a pub in the heart of the city of London, two business owners involved in a conversation not about money, or the next deal, or work, but the benefits of being more compassionate and kind.

You might be surprised that two financial planners are getting together and find themselves talking about kindness. Knowing the best of our particular profession I'm less surprised. I know I find myself having much deeper conversations with my clients that go way past a purely financial conversation.

Often my conversations with clients are about what makes life worth living and I believe that helping your fellow man and woman has to be part of that particular mix. Therefore, in my own experience, good quality financial planners tend to have far broader conversations with the people they work with that include kindness as part of the mix.

I also believe that more people than you believe are on their own mission of intentional kindness and the day after my conversation with Dominic allowed me an insight into how other people are on their own mission of kindness.

In mid-October our business ran an event. We ensured that everyone who attended the event went away with a goody bag which included a pen, a little gadget which helped prop up their mobile, some chocolates and candies and a nice bag to carry it all.

We invited a number of our clients, professional partners and people we like and generally support our business along to join us for the event and while we provided goody bags for all attendees about half of the attendees decided not to take a bag.

This meant there were 50 really nice pens which didn't get taken by our guests. So, the day after my conversation with Dominic in the pub I found myself in the city office we use for meetings (which was also the venue we ran the event). I asked the facilities team at the London office for the pens back and was guided to where the pens were but, before I took the pens away to distribute to our clients, Louis, the facilities manager of our London home came over to chat.

Louis is one of those guys I have an immense amount of respect for. He's an incredibly nice guy, an extremely hard worker and, what I found out on this particular day, is a man who goes above and beyond to help out others, not only professionally but also personally.

"Chris," he said "Can I ask a favour?"

"No worries, Louis," I replied, "How can I help?"

"Every year I fly back to my home town in Guatemala," he started, "and I like to bring back the children in my village a gift."

"It's not much," he continued modestly, "just some paper, some highlighters - and a pen. Each time I go I like to do more. I started doing this a few years ago and I started taking one big bag of gifts. The following year it was two and now it's up to three"

"I was just wondering," he said, "Whether you'd be happy to donate these spare pens? It's just the kids absolutely love the little gift pack and I'd like to make sure I help kids as much as possible."

For me, people like Louis are inspirational to meet. People who selflessly take action and go out of their way to help those less fortunate. A modest man who doesn't make a big deal about his kindness, but quietly takes action by taking something we might consider a trinket and provides it to people who truly value a simple pen as a valuable gift.

"Take them," I said to Louis, "Take them all - and let me know if there is anything else I can do to help."

Sometimes kindness is an intentional action. However, often you get the chance to help someone else's own particular journey as they try to make the world a slightly kinder place

This small act of kindness on my part also made me chuckle. You see all of the pens were branded for my business and it made me smile thinking about a young boy in Guatemalan village wondering why he's using the pen of a financial planning firm based in London!

I also realised that in retrospect I should have thanked Louis. There are certain people who, without realising it, make a difference in your life. Louis highlighted the fact that there's no excuse for not being more kind. It's an intentional choice.

It was an absolute honour to help Louis in such a simple way, but for me the insight that there are others on their own quiet kindness projects reignited the desire for me to continue.

Helping Louis out was one small way I had the chance to help and I'm fortunate enough to get to help in these small ways really often.

If you're reading this then you're likely able to help out too. If it's fundraising by running, swinging or participating an event which involves getting a bunch of you involved in some online quizzing or even if it's helping out by giving something small there are plenty of ways you can become more charitable. Like Danielle you can spend your pre-Christmas period delivering presents around the country to kids' hospices or collecting small gifts for people who aren't so fortunate, there's always something you can do.

So, why not find something you really believe in today, a cause really close to your heart and see if you can be more charitable. I'm sure you'll feel a million times better because of it.

In the next chapter I want to talk about a subject, which as

Brits, is often taboo, but when used correctly can deliver unimaginable amounts of good. I'm talking about money - your own personal cash and, if you can afford to do it, how you might use it to help other people as much as you can.

Chapter 5
Using money for good

It's mid December 2016 and, in a mid-western city in America an 85 year old man was drafting a letter to a friend.

The letter, printed with a straightforward unstuffy letterhead, started simply...

Dear Bill and Melinda,

And after a couple of paragraphs of carefully thought through introduction the letter continues with the following:

It's now been ten years since what my children call 'The Big Bang', the day in 2006 when I made pledges to the five foundations, including yours. Having hit that milestone I thought you might enjoy writing a look backward and forward..."

Now if I told you that the midwestern town our octogenarian friend was writing this particular letter was Omaha, Nebraska would you know who I'm speaking of?

If you're still not sure who I'm writing about here's another clue...

The letter was written by the second wealthiest American to the most wealthy.

Of course, I'm talking about the letter Mr Warren Buffet wrote to Mr Bill Gates and his wife Melinda.

In 2006 Mr Buffet (then the world's richest man) gave away a chunk of money to the foundation that Bill and Melinda Gates set up to support some of the most needy individuals in the world.

While donations to foundations are all relative, the founder of the investment firm Berkshire Hathaway's donation was the largest on record.

A whopping £1.5 billion pounds with a promise to continue to donate in future years. In fact, Mr Buffet has upheld his promise with his most recent donation was a donation of his company's shares worth 3.17 billion back in July 2017.

Now the interesting thing is the letter Bill and Melinda Gates wrote an open letter back. Ane you can read this letter in its whole awesomeness here:-

https://www.gatesnotes.com/2017-Annual-Letter

The most fascinating for me is how Buffet and Gates, two of the richest individuals on the planet, talk not about the value of financial wealth, but the (particularly unique) opportunity they have to change lives.

In the opening paragraphs of his letter of reply Bill Gates talks about the fact that 'while philanthropy isn't business, there are numbers we work with closely to measure and guide our process'.

In the following few pages the founder of Microsoft explains the huge impact he has made in so many people's lives, specifically in improving the health of the poorest in our world - and the numbers are eyewatering. When I say eyewatering, they are so incredibly moving when I first read the reply from Gates to Buffet it made me cry.

You see since 1990 the foundation has saved one hundred and twenty two **million** children's lives.

It's contributed to a worldwide improvement in vaccine coverage where we now vaccinate 86% globally. Also this growth in vaccination has been positive for the economy of these countries too, with each dollar spent on vaccinations generating 44 dollars in economic benefits.

The letter to Buffet contains a bunch of these really encouraging statistics and is certainly worth reading in full for a couple of reasons.

Firstly, it shows that, even in philanthropy both Bill and Melinda Gates focus on measuring the results of the money. Understandably they want significant 'bang for their buck' and are going to spend time measuring the results of their contributions and making changes accordingly to ensure the most benefit for everyone their work impacts.

And

Secondly, it smashes the perception that people who have attained a certain level of financial security (and certainly both Gates and Buffet have exceeded this level some time ago) and have thrived in a primarily capitalist society continue to have concerns, primarily focused on continuous accumulation of wealth.

It's interesting.

Social scientists have shown that excessive wealth can have a detrimental impact on our ability to be kind with several studies showing that those with less money tend to be more empathetic and compassionate.

However, the example Gates, Buffet and many others have set is that actually there are plenty of wealthy socially-minded individuals. These people have a massive positive impact on the world in a wide range of ways by using their money as a force for good. Not only by donating it to causes they believe in, but also making sure the money they invest is being used in the most socially responsible way possible.

You don't need to have Buffet or Gates level of wealth to make decisions designed to make sure your money is being used for good. There are individuals with all different levels of wealth, of all different ages, in countries across the world who have decided that there is power in choosing where to save, spend, invest and potentially donate their money to ensure they're making a positive impact in the world.

For me there are three clear categories when it comes to using money for good.

Firstly, how do you spend your money to do good. This means choosing to buy the products and services you need from businesses who look after their people, value diversity, care for the planet and show they otherwise share your concerns.

Secondly, how do you invest so that you are both rewarding yourself with decent levels of growth, but also by choosing companies to invest in that are more likely to build, hire and sell in a way that makes a positive impact in the world.

Lastly, if you've got enough money for you and your family's needs and, if you choose to do so, how do you give money to causes and organisations that further your values? It might be to support environmental protection, child welfare, historic preservation or any of the hundreds of other issues that need addressing in our world.

I want to explore these three areas and our special guide through the subject of 'Money for Good' is Lauren Janus. Lauren is the Chicago-based Chief Operating Officer and philanthropic advisor at Phīla Engaged Giving, a philanthropic advising firm serving families and foundations. Lauren was a guest on Episode 62 and 63 of *The Kindness Project*.

Lauren has spent a decent amount of time in the charity

sector both in the UK and in the USA. She has a master's degree in international relations and an MBA from the University of California; you could argue that one of these qualifications is amazingly impressive, but both is frankly showing off!

Throughout this chapter Lauren will share what she's learned about using money for good through work. So let's start with looking at how we might be able to spend money to support good work.

Spending for good

From where we do our weekly or monthly 'big shop', to where we choose to spend our leisure time and all the way through to where we get our daily coffees, we make decisions about where and how to spend our hard-earned money every single day of the week.

According to research by the Co-op, the growth in the UK's 'ethical economy' (where people make ethical decisions on what they buy) has increased almost four-fold from 11.2 billion in 1999 to 41.1 billion in 2019. The majority of the changes in how people buy relate to how they buy food and drink and spend money on their homes.

I'm assuming that trying to make sure every purchase you make is as ethical as possible could get pretty frustrating and time-consuming. However, there are a few ways we can all make small subtle changes to support businesses that have an environmental consciousness. Let's look at these changes where we've seen the biggest trends in the past twenty years:-

Ethical Food and Drink

In 1999 when the Cooperative first started their research

they found that the market for ensuring we make ethical purchases for what we put in our mouths existed, but was small - coming in at a billion pounds a year. While that sounds a lot it's actually estimated to be just over 1% of the total spend on shopping each year.

However, in the past twenty years the amount spent on ethically-sourced food has blossomed in popularity. This includes free range eggs, ethically produced bananas and food produced in a way that works in alignment with the environment, as opposed to actively destroying it, One of the greatest areas of growth is the popularity of Fairtrade labelled food.

Fairtrade is a global, UK based, non-profit that focuses on making it easy for consumers to understand that their food has been ethically sourced through the use of the *Fairtrade Mark*.

Fairtrade has made a massive impact on the world by setting standards to make sure that the producers of the food we eat every day are paid fairly, work safely and do less damage to the environment when producing their food. While not a perfect indicator of 'kind' food it's a sign that both the farmers who produce Fairtrade-labelled goods and the retailers who stock it are committed, in some way, to a more ethical method of food production.

According to the Cooperative Ethical Consumerism study, the amount we spent in 2020 on ethically produced food and drink was £14 billion, twenty times the amount we spent twenty years ago. Although this still only accounts for just over 22% of the money we spend on groceries every year, it's still significant progress.

My favourite statistic is the fact that we spend nearly £300 million pounds on Fairtrade bananas alone in the UK - although I'm pretty sure about half of that spend is in our house. I've often described the going-ons in my home as visiting the monkey cage in the zoo and I think our over excessive banana consumption goes a long way towards proving that argument.

There are loads of practical ways you can buy groceries for good.

- Look out for the Fairtrade logo on the food you buy

- Pick a supermarket that you believe has the right values when it comes to procuring food. Try to avoid food waste

These are just a few you can put in place immediately to support the move towards a kinder way to purchase our favourite breakfasts, lunches, dinners and snacks.

Our ethical homes

For many of us, focusing our time, effort and energy on ensuring that our homes are as green as possible makes sense for a couple of reasons. Firstly, it's the right thing to do and, secondly, making changes about how we power and heat our homes is a great way to save a few pounds too.

According to the energy saving trust you can save up to £340 every year by choosing an energy efficient boiler over one that isn't. While energy efficient bulbs are slightly more expensive than normal bulbs, they use a significantly lower amount of energy over time and generally last a lot longer.

Also we can choose the energy efficiency of every single electricity using appliance in our homes at the point of purchase. From our washing machines, tumble dryers, dishwashers, fridges and freezers, you can see how energy efficient all white goods are as they are required to show their energy rating on the label.

Also, one of the easiest things we can do is to reduce waste in our homes is to second hand homeware instead of buy new. The other side of that is to give your old stuff away instead of simply throwing it out. We've got some lovely second-hand items in our home and my wife, Cassie, has an amazing skill which involves being able to, usually in less than an hour, find someone who wants something we don't want or need in the house anymore.

It's true what they say about one man's junk being another man's treasure, even if that treasure is a broken eighteen-year-old TV, half an Ikea cabinet or an old car tyre someone wanted to re-purpose as a swing for their back garden.

Travelling ethically

One of the biggest changes in the past couple of decades has been the way we travel.

In the past few years there's also been massive growth in the use of electric and low fuel consumption vehicles than ever before. As technology gets better and cheaper, the ability to charge your electric car on the road becomes easier as infrastructure improves and government incentives make using a non-petrol car more practical than ever before.

However, in the past 20 years in the UK more and more of us are jumping on our bikes, and spending more and more time each year doing it. In 1999 we spend 298 million on our two-wheeled, human-powered travelling contraptions and this has increased over 300%, as we now spend over 900 million on bikes.

One thing the research doesn't mention is whether this figure includes the amount of lycra purchased by these cyclists, as the amount of cyclists I see on the road with this attire could account for at least half of the increase!

It'll be interesting to see how the recent pandemic will impact how we travel longer-term. While I'm a fan of travelling to experience the world, I do wonder whether we'll be a bit more conscious about how we travel in the future and whether we'll start to see some travel as unnecessary. Time will tell.

One thing we can do is to spend a little bit of time focusing on how we travel. This might be to take one less work related flight (and meet virtually instead), or bike to the office instead of taking the car, or drive to one less meeting. Those small bite-sized changes will contribute to a more positive and sustainable environment.

The other massive area of growth in sustainable and ethical travel is the growth in alternative fuel vehicles which is the name for any automobile not running just on petrol and includes hybrid, electric and solar powered vehicles.

With this market growing from 3 million to 3 billion in twenty years, this has been quite a significant increase. The trend for electric vehicles in particular is growing as the technology improves and the infrastructure designed to support electric grows.

Investing for good

Let's start with a question -

Where is your money invested?

At this point it doesn't matter whether you've got £12.50 in an old pension scheme or a few million quid in a wide range of investment vehicles. Did you know if the money you invest owns shares in or is lent to companies that have a positive or negative impact on the world.

If you're like most people you probably don't.

However over the past few years there has been a slowly growing interest in investors wanting to understand a bit more about where their money is invested and, not only whether this money is growing as they want it to, but also if it's making a positive contribution to the world.

This interest has meant that there has been a more intense focus on what financial professionals call 'sustainable investing', although it has a wide range of names including 'responsible investing', 'impact investing' or 'socially responsible investing'.

The argument for this method of investing your money is simple. This amount of money if we added every single pound we all have in pensions in Great Britain was £6.1 trillion in 2018. That's 61 **million million** pounds - £61,000,000,000,000.

Now I know that I personally struggle when putting super large numbers into some form of perspective so let me explain. If I put six million pounds on every seat in the 02, Twickenham, Wembley arena, AND at every premiership football stadium not only would I have a significant number of happy music, rugby and football fans but that would have just about used up my 6.1 trillion.

In any language that's a decent chunk of cash and the idea of investing for good is that, potentially, this financial clout can be used to invest in companies who have a positive or zero impact on the world. At its purest your investment has the capability to have a significant positive impact on the world.

Socially responsible investing is about not only investing in companies due to their ability to earn investors' money, but also to consider the impact a company might have on the environment, or how it treats its staff or how well it's managed, and whether it's product or service contributes positively or negatively to society. Typically this means focusing on three main areas of how a company behaves.

Environmental

This is how a company impacts our world. While it's never cut and dried, there are certain things businesses can do that contribute positively or negatively to our world.

Let's take one particular example. palm oil.

It's used in everything from ice cream to Instant noodles; from crackers to margarine, not forgetting cosmetic products like shampoo, soap and lipstick.

The problem with products which use palm oil is that, typically, it grows in tropical rainforests. To gather this economically, tons of rainforests are torn down and the rate and pace at which this is happening is scary.

Research from non-profit Rainforest Rescue shows that the equivalent of 300 football fields of forest is destroyed every hour.

As you might know trees are amazing at absorbing carbon dioxide and rainforests are also the home of many different animals. This means that tearing down these forests not only contribute to global warming, but also means destroying the habitats of many animals with 0rangutans in Indonesia being on the verge of extinction due to deforestation - and many other species already extinct.

Before we get too despondent, it's probably worth taking a look at a company that is making a positive environmental impact on the world.

There are plenty of companies that are making fundamental changes to their business model in order to reduce their negative impact on the planet. These strategies include moving towards cleaner sources of energy, using more sustainable or recyclable materials and removing more harmful ingredients (like palm oil) from their products.

There are also the firms that are making improvements in many ways to benefit the environment.

These eco-innovators are doing all sorts of good stuff, including:

- Building systems that re-use more natural water

- Designing more eco- friendly consumer goods

- Making recycling more efficient.

I'm not sure how deep your knowledge is of recycling processing, water efficiency and how to make building products to reduce the impact on the environment.

If you're anything like me it's the depth of a puddle on a particularly dry day.

However what I do know is there are plenty of firms doing great work improving our collective impact on the environment…and you can now choose to invest more of your money into companies doing this sort of work.

Social

How a company treats the people who they employ, work with or are their customers is an important indicator of how judge a business doing good.

For instance, if you were interested in making sure your money was being used for good, you might want to avoid a firm with a reputation for shoddy treatment of their employees.

Also, you might not want to invest (either at all or as much) in a company that might be perfectly reasonable employers, but uses sweat shops to drive down the cost of production.

There's also a decent argument for not investing your hard-earned cash in firms that might make a good profit, but whose main product is designed to hurt, maim or kill indiscriminately. I don't know about you, but I think it's important to make sure that not a penny of my investments are in firms used to create weapons designed to injure or murder. I would not tough businesses that make cluster grenades, biological weapons or land-mines.

Thankfully, there are plenty of fund managers (the people who usually invest your money on your behalf) who won't touch firms like this, but it's probably worth checking out.

While I think we can all agree that companies that produce indiscriminate weaponry might be on most of our 'firms not to invest in' list, there are also companies who have a negative societal impact you may also want to avoid. These might include either firms that produce cigarettes or other tobacco-based products, firms that make most of their cash from gambling or excluding all firms that produce any form of weapons.

A lot of these decisions are clearly moral issues and your perspective on 'investing for good' is probably different from mine, your next door neighbour's or your Uncle John. However, the important thing to remember is that investing for good means you need to consider many of these issues.

While the social impact your investments make is the first step, the next one is to think about how your investments can make the world a better place for the people who live in it.

You might choose to invest in companies who improve medical coverage in countries needing it the most or provide solutions that allow more of us to be immunised from disease. It might be firms that support the delivery of education, or provide financial service in places where access to a local branch of your high street bank might be particularly difficult, or expanding access to technology.

Governance

Good governance simply means running a company well.

You would probably choose not to invest in firms involved in bribery and corruption. Companies who are, to be perfectly frank, a 'bit dodgy'.

On the positive side you may choose to invest in companies who have good systems and processes, who have transparent and fair accounting methods, and firms with no clear conflict of interests.

It's also about considering the make-up of the board and whether a particular firm has individuals on it that might provide a particular perspective. For instance, how many women, or people from minority backgrounds, are involved in the senior management?

You might argue that a bunch of middle-aged white blokes can run a business perfectly well and argue that diversity might not be important. I suppose it depends on the bunch of middle-aged white blokes who are in charge of the company, but I'd also argue that more diversity in a company's senior management team is important. It provides a broader perspective.

Recent research by consulting firm McKinsey suggests that more diverse companies have better financial performance. Companies that have people of all colours and a reasonable balance of both sexes perform 25% better than firms in the same sector and of the same size that don't.

In addition, recent evidence from the Peterson Institute for international Economics highlights that adding women to an executive board increases net margin significantly - an amazing increase of 15% increase in profitability for a typical firm surveyed.

This means the wealth that you've built to become financially stable can still make profits from your investments and also do good, supporting your beliefs.

Historically, there were plenty of reasons for investing in this way, but they weren't particularly popular, at least in the UK. This was due to both the cost of investing this way and the performance of these investments compared to 'normal' investments. However, as the popularity of impact investing grows, the market continues to improve with better value products. This means you can do good and feel good about how you invest your hard earned cash.

This book isn't about investing, and while I'm qualified to deliver financial advice in the UK, nothing in this particular book is designed to give you advice on how to invest or whether impact or sustainable investing is right for you.

However, if you're trying to be kinder to the planet, it's worth considering a change in the way you invest to ensure your money is doing good. I believe knowledge is power - and there is a veil of mystery over investing, so I'm going to consider with a little basic education so you can make decisions from a position of being informed.

There are three main forms of investing for good and it's important to understand these to choose which style might be best for you.

ESG Integration is a method of investing broadly and widely at a relatively low cost, but with more of a tilt towards companies doing good in the world.

For many of these type of funds this still means that you'll be invested in a lot of companies, potentially including some that might not be focused on good, but with more of your money being invested with companies that do.

This approach might allow you to invest more in companies that do good without moving too far away from a conventional evidence-based investment approach.

Socially Responsible investing only invests in companies that either meet a minimum standard of good behaviour or chooses to exclude firms that are, in the fund manager's opinion, particularly naughty.

This might mean that only companies that meet minimum standards in good management are invested in. However, this could also mean that certain sectors, like companies which manufacture nuclear weapons, are automatically excluded as a part of the process.

Impact investing is a process of selecting the companies that are actively making a positive impact in the world and investing in these companies.

Typically, this approach means you invest in a smaller number of companies than any of the other approaches and is usually a more expensive way to invest. But it certainly has more focus on ensuring your money is being used actively for good, even though you're sacrificing the profit levels of a broader spread of assets and lower costs.

There's plenty of research on the companies who invest in this way with each firm investing for good in their own unique style. It's worth doing plenty of due diligence to pick the right impact investment provider or engaging a professional to help you do this.

The reason I mention this is to highlight something important. Your money, and how you choose to use it, has power. Intrinsically, we understand that where we choose to spend and the companies we choose to spend with has an influence if done collectively. However, what we sometimes neglect is the money we're all saving for our financial futures and where these funds are invested has a massive potential to change things for the better.

Now the challenge you've got with any sort of 'investing for good' is that it's not a cut and dried affair.

As we become more conscious of both the impact of our money being used for good AND also the potential investment options that allow us to make a positive impact. There's plenty of investments that say they only invest in companies that meet certain standards, but not all of these reflect what every individual feels is their idea of investing for good.

We've all got a different view on what good investing and good companies look like. I always recommend that, if you think investing for good is for you, it's worth looking under the bonnet to make sure that what you're investing in truly reflects where you want your money to be invested.

One other important thing to consider: there's no such thing as perfect when investing for good. During 2020 and 2021 I spent 18 months researching the market to make sure I could offer a way for my clients to invest for good.

While I'm comfortable with the proposition we built for our clients and think the research we did was pretty robust, I'm also cautious that there is no 'perfect' only the best match we can make.

So, if you do want to invest for good, make sure you do your research to confirm you're comfortable with where your money is actually invested.

Giving for good

I don't know about you, but every time I hear the word 'philanthropy' it sounds like something only the ultra, ultra-wealthy do. This often results in an art gallery, hospital wing or charity being named after them. However, while philanthropy often feels like something for the super-rich, the reality is that we've all got the opportunity to be philanthropic in our own unique way.

All philanthropy means is the ***'desire to promote the welfare of others, expressed by the generous donation of money to good causes'.*** Effectively, it's using money to help others. It's using our money to be kind to our fellow man.

While philanthropists like Bill Gates and Warren Buffet can make donations of hundreds of millions of pounds, the reality is that the donations we all make have the chance to benefit our fellow man in ways large and small.

One of the best things I've ever done is sponsor the kit for my local kids football team. It provided me the opportunity to support a great cause and, while I'm not tackling the big issues like Mr and Mrs Gates and Mr Buffet, I'm helping out in my own little way for something I care about.

If you've got a direct debit giving away a few pounds a month to a cause you know does amazing work then you're a philanthropist.

If you run a business and you raise money for a local charity, or like we do in our business, support causes that help local people - then you're a philanthropist.

And

If you've got something written in your will to give away a proportion of your money to great causes when you're not here anymore - then you're a philanthropist.

One of the greatest challenges we all have, if we're trying to use our money to do good in the world, is how and where we use our money to make the most positive impact.

The good news is that our expert guide through the subject of 'Money for Good', Lauren, is a bona fide expert in helping people make decisions designed to ensure they make the right philanthropic decisions for them - and Lauren's top tip, if you're thinking about how and where to start thinking about giving your money away. Is:

Find something you truly care about.

Think about the things you really care about. Think about how and why you've donated to charities before (and even if it's only been a small donation in the past, most of us have made a contribution to a charity at some point in our lives), and the reasons you felt compelled to donate to this charity.

In addition to this, I'd like to make a small suggestion. I've got a client who uses this amazing phrase:

> *"I'd like to leave the world a better place*
> *when I leave than it was when I arrived."*

His definition of leaving the world a better place will be different to yours, but the answer to the way you might potentially leave the world a better place might provide some of the answers to how you might want to be philanthropic.

I chatted with Lauren about some of the challenges with being philanthropic and mentioned 'The I word'. You see I've had conversations with people in the past where they'd love to make a decent donation to a charity, but they're worried about the money making a direct positive IMPACT on the world.

However, Lauren mentioned that there's actually a really practical way people can assess how effective their contribution could be **www.givewell.org** provides plenty of free information to inform your choice of charities. This identifies charities that have been shown to have a high impact without significant amounts of donations being lost in admin costs.

Where there's a will - there's an opportunity to give

In the UK the super-generous UK public donate about 10 billion pounds every year.

What many people don't realise is that just over 30% of that (3 billion quid) comes from people leaving gifts to charities in their will.

Will gifting is a great way to make sure your good cause gets your financial support when you've passed on, so you leave a small legacy behind.

The good news is that you can choose any amount or any proportion of your wealth and make sure this gets designated in your will. Better still, if your estate is over the threshold of the point where your beneficiaries pay inheritance tax, they won't pay any tax on the money you gift.

The other thing worth considering is that, if you give 10% of your net estate to your charity, it reduces your remaining tax bill by 10% meaning you pay a rate of 36% instead of the usual 40%. Depending on when you read this, the figures may have changed and I'd always suggest you get professional advice if you're planning to do this.

If you're not comfortable with giving large chunks of money away while you may need it, you can be more relaxed with a proportion of your money going to amazing causes in the event of your death.

The interesting thing is that, according to the organisation *Remember a Charity*, only 6% of people leave a gift to charity in their will. They also estimate that if this increased to 10% this would add an additional £1 billion for good causes. Imagine the difference that small increase could make. One billion pounds being used by charities across the UK to continue their fine work.

So, let me make a suggestion. If you haven't made a will yet, get one sorted out and, while you're at it, consider making a donation to a charity. If you've written a will that you haven't looked at for a while, consider including a donation to charity in it. Many of us want to make sure that your family receives the lion's share of whatever you've got left, but if you can allocate any amount, however, small, to give to a cause particularly close to your heart you'll be doing an act of kindness that will, literally live on after you.

What's your legacy?

One of my favourite phrases is 'memento mori' a Latin phrase, which simply means 'remember death'.

Remembering that one day I'm not going to be alive allows me to consider two things. Firstly, the fact that the time I'm going to spend on the planet is finite. It will end. Guaranteed. Because of this I want to make the best of it.

It also means that I want to make sure that when I'm not around my 'echo' can still be felt. In the memories I leave with the people I love and who love me and the good I can do both while I'm still around, as well as when I'm not around anymore. Using my money for good is part of this both now and in the future.

It's important to remember that there's clearly a balance. A balance between making sure you achieve your own financial goals and making sure your money has a positive impact in the world.

That balance is between making sure you use your money for you and your family to live the life you want and helping other people. That balance is different for all of us. However, one thing that has certainly made me happier, and more comfortable with the fact that one day I won't be here anymore, is the fact that I spend some of my money on helping others.

Could you do the same?

Chapter 6
When kindness means business

Business people come in all shapes in sizes. From the one-man-band tradesman, who is the backbone of our economy, to the directors of organisations who employ thousands of people, there are millions of us in the UK and hundreds of millions globally who run businesses.

The latest numbers from the UK government state that there are just under 6 million enterprises in the UK the lion's share of which are small businesses.

Regardless of the shape or size of the business you own or work for, it's fair to say that the primary reason any business exists is to make a profit. You won't get any argument from me on that particular point. I believe that if you're running a business that isn't consistently profitable you're probably not running a business, but have an expensive hobby. So making a profit isn't anything any business owner or leader should apologise for.

I also believe that businesses have a fantastic opportunity to contribute towards a society where we're all a little bit kinder to each other. Not only that, but businesses, from the smallest to the largest, play a fundamental role in living in a society where we're all a bit better to each other.

There are people who will argue that businesses can't be kind. If the core role of business is to make a profit then there's a dichotomy between being kind and making money. I know this is not true and in this chapter I'll share why.

In addition, I want to give you some ideas to make either

the business you own or the place you work a slightly kinder place and share some stories of the amazing individuals we've interviewed who run their businesses in a way that contributes to the world in positive ways.

Before we start exploring all these areas let's try to answer a more fundamental question...

Can businesses be kind?

Businesses can be run in many different ways. I know there are plenty of financially successful businesses whose owners and managers believe that their primary objective is to make as much profit as possible. Fortunately, most business owners take a more subtle and nuanced approach

I think one of the major contributory factors in running a successful business long-term, however you define success, is maintaining relationships of trust. Trust with your customers or clients, trust with your suppliers or professional partners and trust with your teams.

When trust is lost bad things happen and it's often an uphill struggle for companies to recover. Ask Enron, or Volkswagen, or any of the banks embroiled in shoddy behaviour in the past couple of decades.

I like Marc Benioff's, one of the co-founders of Salesforce, take on business when it comes to this particular point.

> *"Every CEO needs to ask themselves. What is the most important thing for your company? What is your highest value? I know at Salesforce our highest value is trust. Nothing is more important than the trust we have with our customers, or*

employees, or partners or our top
executives."

We've all seen what happens when companies break this relationship of trust. Volkswagen's focus on short-term gains and lying about the outcomes of their carbon dioxide testing had a massive impact on their share price, but perhaps more importantly an even bigger impact on the longer-term reputation of their business.

While trust and kindness in business aren't the same, I suggest that these two concepts are interconnected. I believe that applying the principals of practical kindness in our business, not as a cynical way to build trust, but because you genuinely want to build a sustainable business to be proud of. One that not only makes money, but also contributes to the world, will lead to deeper more sustainable relationships of trust with its customers and, potentially, a better business for the future.

Life is often complex and there are decisions to be made that aren't particularly straightforward. However, if you believe that trust is the foundation for better, long-term sustainable business, then thinking about how we can be kinder to each other will play a fundamental part in doing this.

While you can clearly run a profitable and financially successful business without kindness at its core, business leaders, shareholders and everyone employed in businesses across the world has an opportunity to both make money and make our world a better place.

There's plenty of business advice out there talking about how to achieve success in business. Most of what we see about business tells us that increased success is defined as more revenue, more growth and more profits.

However, it doesn't take much to understand that there are a plenty of examples that show businesses are capable of doing well **and** doing good.

Doing well and doing good where your values are at the core of the business.

If you run a business you've worked hard to build yourself you might be familiar with this journey.

When I started my business the first couple of years were all about survival. With my only previous experience being in situations where I knew my salary was going to be paid starting a business was a bit of a shock to the system.

At the time Charlotte was only six, I had a mortgage to pay and an intense pressure that I couldn't let either Cassie or Charlotte down. However, it was clear that Charlotte didn't quite understand how setting up a commercial enterprise worked.

I remember the day I'd decided to leave paid employment and go it alone and told Cassie who, while concerned, had faith I'd be able to make it work (something I'd have been unable to do without the amazing support Cassie continues to give me). Charlotte was less impressed. I remember a conversation with her in her bedroom when I'd enthusiastically and excitedly told her I was 'leaving my job and starting a business' and she'd responded by bursting into uncontrollable inconsolable tears.

"Oh darling," I remember saying, "What's the problem?"

"Dad, if you've left your job who's going to pay for the holidays?"

This still makes me chuckle now, but at that time I wasn't 100% certain that holidays were going to be at the top of the list of household expenses. After a couple of years we built a decent reputation, brought some lovely clients on board and started to build the business.

Then I started thinking about sustainability. How can we build a business that sustains through ups and downs and has the ability to continue to survive commercially. While this is a constantly evolving and changing challenge, we spent a few years exploring the best way to do this.

A few years ago I started to think about what my business really meant. Did it exist as purely a money making entity or did it exist as an extension of me, what I believe and a reflection of my values?

I certainly didn't believe that my business existed just to make money and the more I thought about the particular question it raised another. What did I truly believe?

Coming from the corporate world meant that I'd always been surrounded by conversations about corporate values. To be perfectly frank talking about values in a lot of the organisations I'd been part of always felt empty. Words that sounded good, but felt empty. Something that companies and larger organisations felt they had to do, but didn't walk the talk when it came to action.

As my business evolved I started to think about values in a different light. After all, if my business could be about more than just a money making entity what would it be? What COULD it be?

I decided to keep it simple and base our values as a business of my own personal values. They're the values I live by and the values I teach Sophie and Charlotte. My own values are:

- Have fun (what's life about if you're not enjoying it?!)

- Be fair

- Focus on improvement

and one particular value that underpins the other three -

- **Do well and do good**

I believed that it was possible to run a business that 'did well'(was profitable and commercially sustainable) andt also did a decent amount of good.

Our endeavours as a relatively small business are modest in comparison to what larger businesses can achieve, but we're certainly trying to do what we can to practically help and that manifests itself in a few different ways. We:

- Sponsor a local kids football team

- Deliver financial education to schools

- Run a bunch of charity events where we invite our professional connections along to fundraise

- Run events designed to raise as much as we can for a particular cause.

...and it turns out that we're not alone. When you look for businesses doing good they're easy to find

There are plenty of organisations, large and small, doing exactly the same - and businesses who from day one put 'doing good' at the forefront of everything they do.

One of my favourite examples is TOMS, an innovative shoe retailer. They're a fantastically successful business with 'doing well and doing good' hardwired into their business model. TOMS was founded on a simple principal; for every pair of shoes sold, another pair will be donated to someone who really needs them.

This principal, so simple but so powerful, has resulted in massive success for this particular business. There will be plenty of insight into why this particular business has done fantastically well, but here's my take. When you buy a pair of TOMS shoes you're not just buying a pair of shoes. You're choosing to support a cause. You're choosing to pay more to give back. You're choosing to do well and do good and support TOMS to do the same.

Not everyone will choose to do this. Many will choose to buy Reeboks, or Skechers, or Nikes. However, if you find enough people happy to support what you do it's entirely possible to build a business which truly does well and does good.

The most recent stats show that TOMS has given away 95 million pairs of shoes since their launch. So, that's a business that's clearly helped a lot of people with something many of you reading this will take completely for granted.

However, like many businesses TOMS have had significant challenges, since 2019 they've moved away from the 'buy one to give one model'. However they are clearly a business with a clear focus on combining profit and purpose. This has meant that whilst the 'one for one' model that worked for many years has now evolved so that TOMS now donates $1/3^{rd}$ of its profits to grassroots organisations doing good in the world.

Their donations have helped people all over the world including India, Paraguay as well as helping the homeless in the UK through the support of Centrepoint.

The interesting thing about the story is how the TOMS model of 'buy one, give one' has spread. Companies have adopted this model to sell toothbrushes, books, soccer balls, soap, socks and knickers.

Then there's B Corp. An organisation that believes in business as a force for good and provides an accreditation, with robust standards, designed to ensure that the businesses who sign up to this organisation are living by these principals.

In the early days of *The Kindness Project* podcast I was lucky enough to persuade fellow financial planner Jeannie Boyle to come and talk to us about why the business she's part of, EQ investors, decided to become a B Corp accredited business.

Jeannie and the team heard about the B Corp movement in the early days and as it started to really grow in the US. She decided, as the standard was being launched in the UK, that it fitted in with how EQ Investors wanted to do business.

The process of becoming a B Corp is a rigorous one and you've got to evidence that you're actually deserving of the 'B Corp' badge. To become a B Corp they look at many different aspects of your business including where you buy and source your goods, how you run your company, how you fairly represent your community, how your business measures and looks to reduce the amount of waste it generates and how your business really measure the positive impact on its clients.

Jeannie has a genuine belief that companies who want to do some good can be very profitable too. The reason? People want to engage with companies who ae actively engaged in doing good in the world…which is the reason the B Corp badge is so powerful.

I've also been lucky enough to speak to many business owners and leaders who put kindness at the heart of everything they do.

Pinky Lilani CBE spends her time not only running her successful food business, Spice Magic, but also sharing her stories of kindness and promoting the leaders from big business who believe the kind leadership is fundamentally important through her annual 'kindness and leadership' awards.

Rebecca Robbins, Global Chief Culture and Learning Officer for Interbrand, the biggest branding agency in the world, whose clients include Mini, Samsung, Santander, BMW and many more.

I met Rebecca at her London office and we spent quite a while chatting about how kindness defines her leadership style. What I learned from Rebecca the most during our interview was why kindness in business can be a smart commercial move (but not always)

However, our conversation didn't start with a conversation about kindness. Our conversation started, as all good chats should, with both Rebecca and I professing our love of Lego.

You see Rebecca hasn't only worked with Samsung, Santander and BMW; she's also worked with Lego!

Once we'd established our love of the little bricks we got down to business and talked about how and why Rebecca felt kindness in business was so important.

We discussed why kindness is so important when thinking about working in teams and talked about a piece of research by Google I'd not heard about before.

We all know that Google performs research all the time. However, what I didn't know is that Google has done research into what makes the perfect team. The research, named 'project Aristotle' (a tribute to the famous Aristotle quote "the whole is greater than the sum of its parts) was to answer one simple question...

"What makes a team really effective at work?"

Google found there were five factors which were really important:

- Having dependable team mates

- Having a clear roles

- Plans and goals

- Doing work that matters to the team and makes a positive impact

- Psychological safety.

The last one underpins all the others. All team members need to feel comfortable enough to communicate openly honestly and have confidence that no-one on the team will embarrass or punish someone for admitting a mistake, asking a question or offering a new idea.

It was found that the way you build a team that has psychological safety is build a kind environment at work. One where everyone is present and curious. An environment where loads of questions are asked with the intention of learning from others. An environment where it's important to be available and approachable,. A place where decision making is made after you ask the opinion of your teammates and an environment where, as a leader, the team feels comfortable sharing their ideas, challenging your ideas and talking about failure openly.

Effectively, Google found that a good work and team environment is an environment where empathy was core to the approach. An environment where people are respectful of each other. An environment where kindness underpins the way the best teams work.

It's important to highlight that the research also found that accountability was important (that's where the dependability and clear goals were vital) but everything was underpinned by creating a culture of psychological safety...basically kindness at work!

So, kindness in a team culture is a smart thing to do, but kindness in business extends a lot further than that.

My conversation with Rebecca was fascinating and wide-ranging and I'd certainly recommend you check it out on the podcast. Although we talked a lot about kindness at work we also explore philosophy, the importance of curiosity, and what we can do to change the culture of business from one where conflict is encouraged to one where collaboration is the route that businesses want to take.

Why commercial kindness needs to be authentic - and what can happen when it isn't.

For companies like TOMS, being a business with kindness at its core has been a smart commercial move. For others it's not worked as well.

One example being when Skechers for one of its ranges, copied the TOMS model. For every pair of shoes sold another pair went to someone in the world who would really benefit. They even called the range 'BOBS' in tribute.

The range was a relative commercial flop. For some reason, while TOMS was seen as a cause to get behind, BOBs was seen as a way to 'market' doing good - in other words to use the kindness just to sell more shoes.

Maybe it was and maybe it wasn't. Maybe the idea was to copy TOMS idea due to its commercial success or maybe someone at Skechers genuinely wanted to do some good. Either way customers didn't buy, in part because it felt more like a marketing ploy than a genuine desire to do good in business.

I believe that if we want to do good in our businesses, and want our clients or customers to buy into our businesses because we're doing good, then it needs to come from a genuine and authentic place.

In today's increasingly connected world full of marketing messages we've become increasingly cynical consumers. We need to believe in the companies we choose to work with and purchase from. Companies who have a powerful reason 'why' at their core and can authentically communicate this have an advantage.

Companies that cynically try to cash in on the idea of kindness as a marketing concept, without truly believing in the power of business doing good as opposed to doing well, might find themselves exposed to negative scrutiny.

Big, medium-sized or small - kindness should be part of every business

All business have the power to be kinder.

From companies like TOMS who have built mighty businesses with kindness at their core, to small boutique businesses like mine who work hard to contribute to their local community.

However imagine this...

There are 45,000 listed businesses in the world, businesses large enough to be traded on a stock exchange. Collectively these businesses employ millions of people. More than 5000 business are listed on UK markets.

In the UK there are also close to 6 million private sector businesses with a (broad) estimation of 295 million private sector businesses worldwide.

Imagine this - 2% of these businesses, regardless of size, made a choice. Once every year they committed to focus on, just for a day and in a way where they could continue to run their business, active and intentional acts of kindness.

If just 2% of businesses did one kind thing in that day (ignoring the 'ripple effect' acts of kindness produce in the UK alone) you'd produce just over 120,000 extra days of kindness, equating to over 17,000 weeks of kindness or 329 extra years of intentionally kind days. Imagine the impact!

The global figure is even more outstanding. 2% of global businesses committing to mobilise their teams to spend a day intentionally performing acts of kindness could potentially provide an additional 16,0000 years of kindness.

Let's talk business. Let's talk death.

One of my favourite phrases, and one that gets often repeated in my house followed by subsequent eye-rolls from all members of my family, is *'Memento mori'*.

'Memento mori' is the Latin version, but it was originally derived from Greek philosophy. The concept is deeply human, which is why similar phrases have popped up in cultures and religious teachings across the globe. In Buddhism it's *maranasati*.

In Japanese Zen culture it's *Hagakure*.

The Tibetan Buddhists call it *Lojong*

And it's been used as the inspiration for art, and writing, and philosophical thought around the world.

The meaning of Memento mori is universal, simple and applies to us all. It simply means.

Remember that you must die.

You might be thinking that this is a morbid thing to think

about. Instead of remembering we're all going to die you might prefer to consider the last time you had a really nice curry, or your favourite flavour of crisp, or even the last time you trod on a piece of Lego (it was a particularly painful red piece designed to be a wheel arch on a London bus), rather than considering the fact that we are all mortal. But I'd suggest that when we think about our lives and what we do with our lives it's important.

When I think about the fact that one day I'm not going to be here anymore, and I happen to believe that's a particularly permanent state, I can't help thinking about a few things.

What do I want to be remembered for?

On my deathbed what do I want to be proud of?

What role model do I want to be for the people who outlast me?

I'm lucky to work with a number of people who have achieved financial independence. They don't need to worry about money too much and trust us to ensure they won't need to in the future. However, I'm also fortunate enough to have conversations with these people about a lot more than money - often including what's really important to them.

Often the first things are family, or travel, or the fact that the work they do contributes to the world. It's interesting to discover that, while financial freedom is important for most of us, the accumulation of wealth for its own sake, is quite a way down that list.

The reality is that we don't exist purely as money making entities. We exist as sons and daughters, as mums and dads, as brothers and sisters. We exist as members of our communities, as friends, as people connected to others. We exist to give proper meaning to our lives - through the stories we tell, or the experiences we go through, or as a result of what we do for other people.

I'm a firm believer that these principles apply to every aspect of our lives. If we run our own businesses being profitable and continuing to grow is important to be sustainable, but to bring more meaning to our work that connects with who we actually are, will ensure that we believe in what we do.

What is the purpose of your business?

Like the purpose of your life isn't just to make money the purpose of your business goes beyond that too. It's important to be profitable, to make money, to continue to grow, but our businesses have the power to be far more than simply a money-making machine.

Businesses, collections of people getting together for a commercial endeavour, have massive power and influence in our modern capitalist society. Your business can have a noble and ambitious vision.

If you're a business leader, owner of an enterprise or have a position of influence you have the power to make the world a better place in any way - **what are you going to do about it?**

What I've loved seeing during the pandemic is plenty of businesses large and small coming together to support the most vulnerable. Not to mention the ordinary people who are front line workers and continue to support our country, while the rest of us stayed safely at home. It's a sure sign that businesses at their best aren't simply money making entities, but have the ability to do more.

8 ways businesses can be kinder

There a plenty of ways businesses can be kinder and I'm going to share 10 ideas you might find useful.

1: Free 'product'

Virtually all businesses have the chance to give away some of their product away free to help the needy. You'll find many large and small companies who do this regularly.

Tesco give away some of food to local foodbanks and charity organisations as well as working with organisations like National network FareShare to ensure this happens.

Tesco's however aren't alone as Sainsburys, Asda, Morrisons and many other food retailers have schemes in place to give away their products to food banks ready to be distributed to the people who need it the most.

An organisation called *In Kind Direct* work with a number of huge businesses, including Amazon, Samsung, Proctor and Gamble, The Disney Store and Adidas UK to distribute their goods to local charities, so the charities can be run cost efficiently as well as benefiting their local communities.

However, there are plenty of businesses who not only provide 'stuff', but their time and expertise to the people who need it the most.

A local hospice runs an annual £50 business challenge, where business owners are given £50 with the aim to use it to make as much money as possible in a specified time-frame. The £50 seed money is sponsored by a local company and, at worst, the Charity gets the seed money back, at best can be converted into many hundreds of pounds by small business owners. The charity gets funds, the business owners learn how to grow small investments into larger ones and feel good about what they're doing too - definitely a win-win.

All over the country the Citizens Advice Bureau provide hours of professional advice on a range of different subjects with much of this advice provided by experts in their field committed to help people on a voluntary and unpaid basis.

Every year, usually in October Financial planners all over the UK, from the large national firms to the smaller boutique practices, give their time and expertise to individuals to help them successfully plan their financial futures.

These are just a handful of examples of the way companies can give the product they might usually sell at a profit for free, in moderation and at the right time, and still continue being profitable.

2: Education

I think often we underestimate the amount we can teach others. Earlier in this book I shared my story of how I used my knowledge to support younger people to understand more about money but my belief is that all of us have something to share. A way to help someone else navigate lifes challenges with a bit more knowledge than they had before.

So, here's the question. What have you learned in the world of work that could help others?

If you're a business owner you've certainly learned skills along your journey that a young person might benefit from. If you're an expert in your particular field, how could you share you skills, knowledge and expertise to support others.

My experience is that educational establishments are keen to share real world experiences with their students. I've personally spoken at schools, colleges and universities with an aim that sharing my experiences will provide insight, knowledge and inspiration to someone looking to make positive changes to their lives.

The reality is that your insights, both through work and through life, will be both valuable and unique and one practical way of helping others through your business is to educate others about what you've learned.

I believe every day is a school day. We never stop learning. We do however sometimes underestimate what we've learned in our lives and careers and I do wonder whether we should focus our time on sharing more of what we've learned.

One of the ways you can definitely be kinder in your business is to donate your time to educate others. This might by speaking, or mentoring. This might be at a school, college or university although it might also be in your own place of business or via a professional body.

I know plenty of experienced professional people who choose to use their time to teach, mentor or speak to the next generation to support them in their journeys and I've never heard any of them regret the change to do this.

As a parent I know that one of the things I want my two daughters to do when they go into their chosen careers is to be inspired by what they do…and how better to do this than listen and learn from someone who can help them understand what this means in practical terms.

Could this be you?

3: Sponsorship

Two of my favourite clients is a couple we've looked after for a few years. Jim and Sylvie are retired book lovers who trust us to look after their money, but also like to pop into the office for a chat every couple of months. This is something I always look forward to as it provides me with an opportunity to chat about books - something I will take every opportunity to do.

However, about a year and a half ago when they popped in, Jim wanted to chat about something specific.

"I'm after a favour, Chris," said Jim. "I've been involved with a kids' football club for a few years and they need new kit. Would you consider sponsoring the club?"

I told Jim I'd think about it and after a pleasurable chat about what Sylvie was currently reading they left to get on with their day and left me to get back to work.

However, as I sat back down at my desk I noticed Cassie was looking at me expectantly. "What do you think?" she said:

"About what?"

"About sponsoring the kids' football team?"

I considered it for a minute and gave an honest answer, "It's not a massive amount of money, but do you genuinely think it'll generate any extra business? I doubt it to be frank."

She looked back with a wry smile, but a determined look in her eye. "That's not really the point, is it? It'll allow us to support the local community, help the kids out as well as helping Jim and Sylvie."

"You're right," I agreed, "Let's do it!"

A couple of weeks later I'm standing in a park. It's drizzly, but bright and there are twenty boys warming up to prepare for a football match.

Jim, a man incredibly sprightly for his age, is busy putting up a goal ready for the match, but then notices me and comes over. "Thanks for coming, Chris - just before we start the team have got a little thank you gift for you."

A few minutes later I'm being presented with a framed shirt proudly emblazoned with the Cervello logo and spent the next hour and a bit proudly cheering on a local boys football team, none of whom I knew, but whom I'm incredibly proud to support...

The Football Association estimates that there are 3.35 million kids across the UK who play football regularly, many of whom play for local clubs. These clubs often couldn't survive without the support from parents donating time, people like Jim who help organise and run these clubs, and local businesses supporting the teams and contribute to the fitness of the children who play, by providing their support.

If you run a business and football sponsorship isn't your bag there are a bunch of different ways you can support your local community. You could sponsor a community group, sponsor a half marathon, or sponsor a local literary, food or music festival as a business. Anything that supports your local community so it can be as amazing possible for the people in it.

4: Giving money and time

Corporate philanthropy is companies, typically larger ones, who contribute to charities and other not-for-profit organisations, in two ways. This might be via a financial donation or a contribution in time.

One of my favourite interviews for *The Kindness Project* has been Tracey Walsh who runs the East End Community Foundation. This organisation is dedicated to alleviating poverty and increasing aspiration in some of the most challenging parts of East London, a part of the world I know well as I was brought up in one of the areas the Foundation supports.

While Tracey has led the East End Community foundation since 2012 she's spent her whole career working in organisations designed to regenerate communities and tackling both inequality and poverty.

We talked about the fact that East London has been a fascinating place to do this work, particularly during a time period where there's been such change in this part in London.

However, what we also talked about was how much of a paradox parts of East London are. For example, Tower Hamlets is the home of Canary Wharf, one of the largest economic zones in Europe and across the road from this display of wealth there are areas with some of the highest levels of deprivation in the country.

The great thing about organisations like Tracey's is that they act as way for all sorts of projects to get funded. For example, if you've got an idea to help the community and you only need a small grant then you can apply for up to £800 to run a community Christmas party, or purchase a computer to help run a small organisation.

On the other end of the scale there are much larger grants issued, which are designed to make a more substantial impact, but require more effort to apply for. Clearly Tracey and her team has an obligation to make sure that there is enough positive impact for the foundation to part with this money.

When we interviewed Tracey it was clear she loves her job. For her the thing that 'gets her up in the morning' was the positive impact of the foundation's work. Tracey spoke about the fact that tailoring the funding the foundation gives out to specifically and positively impact the people they want to support is vital.

The funding for the foundation comes from a wide range of sources. A decent chunk is from large businesses who want to support their commitment to corporate social responsibility all the way through to local residents who want to make a contribution towards supporting their community.

We talked about why these businesses give to a foundation like the EECF and not directly invest in projects in the communities in question. We discussed the fact that investing in the foundation meant that the money could be focused on projects with the greatest impact. When companies simply spend their corporate social responsibility budget in a scattergun way the impact is likely to be less than when they put their investment in the hands of the experts at the foundation.

While some of you reading this will work with larger businesses with budgets designed to do good, Tracey outlined that there are still ways smaller business can help in ways which are both affordable to your business and means you're supporting the people you want to help.

One thing worth considering as a business owner, instead of giving money, is to donate time to support others. In her interview Tracey talks about the fact that the one of the greatest areas you can support others is by simply showing others what's possible with their lives.

Tracey certainly believes that one way to improve aspiration is not only to build skills, but to show what's possible. I know plenty of business people who mentor young people, teach skills and sometimes simply inspire them to think differently about their lives in a way which broadens both their perspective and aspirations.

You've got the power to do this, and in turn inspire the lives of a young person in a meaningful way.

5: Connecting people

When humans first started to work together the resources they shared were basic in nature - crops, food, and skills. Communities were small, but villages grew and over centuries became towns and then cities. Skills became more diverse and the goods and services we could swap and trade morphed from a handful to thousands. Monetary units developed to facilitate this process of exchange system.

The pace of this growth hasn't reduced and as we move forward in the 21st century it's unlikely that this pace won't change anytime soon. Technological innovations has made our world more complex. The mind boggles when you consider what the first European farmers would have made of the profession of pilot or, even stranger, what a Roman centurion would make of a professional Youtuber.

It's unlikely that with the diverse range of skills someone might need in a modern economy you will be able to help everyone with your particular unique set of skills. However, one way we can all be a little kinder to each other, particularly when working within our businesses, is to be a connector. I've experienced the power of this in a number of ways.

Firstly many of the amazing guests we have on our podcast have been introduced by other guests and my experience has been that kind people doing amazing things in the world are really good at connecting people for mutual benefit. I've also made friends, built deep relationships with people I love working with and have learned loads from the introductions made to me. It's why I try to be a better connector.

Being a connector isn't just about networking. It's about wanting to help people, it's about building your professional network, it's about staying in touch, it's about being a trusted resource.

For me being a connector is not only about business. It's about a desire to help and a desire to introducer people you like to other people you like for their mutual benefit. The additional benefit is that the best connectors are among some of the best business people I know. A coincidence? Maybe, but an interesting one all the same.

6: Fundraise

We can all fundraise as individuals, but there is an additional opportunity when we do it within our businesses and workplaces. Through my business we've had the opportunity to see this in action in a few ways.

One way of doing this is via events. A couple of times every year we run an event. Part networking, part social and part thank you to our clients and professional connections. We always include a fundraising element to the proceedings.

Sometimes we beg, borrow and steal some lovely prizes. Sometimes we run a competition to raise money. At one event an amazing professional photographer we know donated his time and sold headshots in exchange for a donation to the charity.

Another way is workplace match funding. If you're an employee and you're raising money for a cause you know does amazing work, it's always worth finding out whether your employer can help you raise more money by effectively matching the money you raise.

Typically it's corporates that provide match funding, but it's always worth asking the question of your employer.

It's also worth noting, if you're an employee or a business owner looking to make a contribution from your business, as I write this, although contributions from a business don't benefit from gift aid, they are considered a business expense and can reduce the amount the business pays in corporation tax.

7: Helping others succeed

One of the things that I do that's most personally satisfying is to help others succeed. Thankfully, I get to do that in exchange for money in my role as a financial planner, but I also spend time in my working week helping people get better outcomes who never pay me a penny and I'm certainly not going to stop now.

From fellow financial planners to young people looking to enter into a financial planning career all the way through to prospective business owners looking not to make the same mistakes I did when I started - there are a million ways you can help others get better at what they do.

This can be coaching or mentoring someone, sharing your skill in a particular task or area - be creative!

8: Saying thank you

The easiest way to spread kindness in our business is simply to say 'thank you'. Two super-simple words that are so powerful at home, in life and especially at work.

Actively looking for ways to say thank you is important and saying thanks more helps us, our teams, our clients and anyone else we work with.

Firstly, saying thanks is good for us. I've already written about the importance of gratitude and this principle applies just as much to our working lives as it does to every single aspect of our experience.

We know that being grateful makes us feel better and it's clear that saying thank you more makes us feel more grateful.

However, saying thanks is also particularly important when it comes to motivation and encouraging teams in your business. According to a relatively recent study, companies who spend just 1% of their payroll budget on thanking and intentionally recognising their employees are more likely to see higher levels of retention and better financial results as a business.

We all want to be rewarded and encouraged and our teams are no different. So, creating a working environment in our businesses where our teams feel rewarded and encouraged is really important. This can start with a simple thank you.

It's also important to share some love with our clients and customers too. The reality is that saying 'Thank you for choosing to work with us' goes a long way. It acknowledges that anyone who chooses to work with you has a choice but also lets them know you sincerely appreciate it.

Let's not forget about all the other people who support us in our working lives. In my business I'm massively grateful for all of the help and support I receive from all of the people who choose to introduce us to their clients, all of the individual who over the years who have given me such good advice (as well as the advice which might have been not so good, but was still well meaning!) and much more.

There are plenty of ways you can say thank you to your teams, clients or customers and connections. It might be as simple as a verbal or written thank you, a card (even a postcard) it might be a gift, or it might be to run an 'appreciation event'.

Whatever way you choose to give thanks for the people you work with I know one thing for sure - they'll appreciate it. When we are thanked we always do.

Chapter 7
The science of kindness

Here's the truth about kindness that nobody talks about:

Kindness is ultimately a selfish act

There may be people who disagree with this concept, and I've certainly had guests on our podcast who disagree with the fact that kindness is selfish, but there's a really simple explanation for why being kind to others is ultimately selfish.

It's good for you!

Throughout these chapters about kindness I've spoken about the physical effects of kindness - and there is quite a lot of information about how what we think and do affects how we feel. I've done some basic research and I'd like to share some of this here.

All of the research points to the fact that being kind to others in all aspects of our lives makes us happier, healthier people and gets all the right kinds of chemicals flowing around our body on a more regular basis. This is something we're going to explore in more detail.

There are plenty of chemicals floating around our body that have a direct impact on our happiness. All these chemicals can be triggered in different ways.

Melatonin helps us sleep well. We can help our bodies to generate melatonin by eating turkey, chicken and, if you prefer your diet to be a bit greener asparagus, olives and grapes.

The modern day phenomenon of artificial light at bedtime plays absolute havoc with melatonin generation. It's one of the reasons that scrolling on your mobile phone when you should be sleeping is a bad idea. It's something we all struggle with; the best strategy is to leave your phone in another room when you're sleeping to remove the temptation.

Research also shows that a nice hot bath can increase melatonin production. A relaxing soak also reduces the stress hormone cortisol.

As with the bedroom, it's probably wise to leave your mobile in another room as, while soaking in a nice, hot bath is really good for you, it's not that great for your phone! Or so I've heard - from a friend.

Endorphins are amazing chemicals and act as the body's natural painkiller. They also relieve stress and make you feel generally well.

You can boost endorphins in a number of ways, including vigorous physical activity and laughing. It's one of the reasons that although throwing myself around a class at my gym isn't a particularly pretty sight, I know it's an incredible way to make me feel better.

There's also some research to show that spicy foods and dark chocolate also release endorphins. However, eating a curry and a Lindt 'extreme dark' chocolate bar during an intense exercise class might be unwise! Although if you do decide to combine these things I would love to come and watch. Maybe even film it.

Endorphins are also generated by volunteering, donating and helping others.

Dopamine is quite often described as the 'happy hormone', but it's a lot more than that. It tells the brain what actions are pleasurable and is involved in a lot of the brain's systems. This includes motor and cognitive function, motivation and reward, decision making, memory and maternal and reproductive behaviours.

Interestingly, there's a balance between too much and too little dopamine. If we have low levels of dopamine this dampens down our enthusiasm and excitement. However, too much dopamine is linked to being overly competitive, aggressive and a lack of impulse control.

If you're aiming to increase your dopamine levels naturally this can be done by eating a healthier diet and doing more activities that make you feel good.

Being actively grateful for our lot in life releases more dopamine, as well as looking back and seeing all of the good things we've done in our lives generates dopamine. If you don't already you might keep a gratitude journal or incorporate a daily few minutes of being grateful into your routine.

Let's not forget **phenylethylamine** and **norepinephrine.** These are neural stimulants, as well as being particularly difficult to pronounce, are responsible for our overall happiness.

There are two specific chemicals generated by our bodies that improve our overall wellbeing and I want to put these in the spotlight.

The reason? As this is a book about kindness, these are the two chemicals that improve our own wellbeing. There's also plenty of evidence that being kind to others is a really effective way to boost the production of these chemicals and, therefore, they make us happier.

Serotonin is a chemical that helps the messages between the nerves and the brain get delivered. It's found mainly in the brain, the blood, and, rather uncomfortably, the bowels.

Serotonin is the postman of the body, responsible for delivering messages between different parts of the body. Therefore, serotonin does a lot, apart from throw packages over your garden gate.

Serotonin impacts every part of the body, including our emotions, sleep, memory, learning and even temperature regulation. Serotonin also helps to reduce depression, regulate anxiety, heal wounds and maintain bone health. Serotonin is the kind of message delivery service that also makes you happier, healthier and helps the body run effectively; like WhatsApp for the body, but a LOT better!

Oxytocin is a hormone and is another chemical that is produced by the brain and is used to transmit messages around the body.

It's informally called the 'love hormone' and tends to increase in your body when we're involved in social activities as well as the more intimate relationships. It is demonstrated well by the phrase 'all loved up' or perhaps., the less complimentary 'can't keep their hands off each other'!

Oxytocin acts as a natural form of antidepressant, increases trust, increases the empathy we feel for others, strengthens our relationships, eases stress, and protects our heart.

Oxytocin triggers feelings of love and protection and naturally occurs when parents and their children look at one another. If we're generating more oxytocin, we build closer relationships, have more empathy with people, have the ability to communicate more positively and improve our social skills.

Now let's be clear. I'm not a doctor. They clearly don't hand out any sort of doctorate for reading a few books about happiness and kindness as well as doing a few hours of internet research. However, there is a doctor who has written a decent amount about kindness.

Dr David Hamilton gained his PhD, worked in the pharmaceutical industry for a few years, but now writes and speaks about kindness in our lives for a living. He is the author of the *Little Book of Kindness*, *The 5 Side-effects of Kindness* and many others.

In the early years of *The Kindness Project* we had the chance to interview David. I had an amazing chat for over an hour with him and realised directly after we finished that I had forgotten to press record!

I've certainly learned a lot both from reading David's books and consuming his online content and I'd recommend you check him out on all of your favourite social media platforms.

I'm also massively gutted that he shared so much during our interview, but I'll never get to share his wisdom. It was one of those 'Doh' moments.

If you're in the mood to read more about the links between kindness and happiness I'd recommend *The 5 Side-effects of Kindness*. In this book David makes a compelling case for everyone to be a bit kinder. He explains why kindness is something we should do to support our own wellbeing and how some of the chemicals that help us to be happier are sparked by being kind.

So how does this work in practice?

Being kind and performing acts of kindness release serotonin and oxytocin in our bodies. These two chemicals make us happier, prevent us from being depressed, ease stress and protect our heart. It's as simple as that.

Now in addition to all of these scientific benefits of being kind, there's also a lot more besides.

- https://www.randomactsofkindness.org/the-science-of-kindness

- In a UC Berkley study around half of participants found that they felt stronger and had more energy after helping others

- Performing acts of kindness can also make you feel less anxious. In a study by the University of British Columbia a bunch of highly anxious people did six acts of kindness per week. After just a month there was a significant increase in positive moods experienced byt the individuals and they were more likely to feel more social.

So here's the logic

One of the best ways to be kind to yourself is to be kind to other people.

After all being kind to others, because of the massive benefits experienced by both you and those you help, is ultimately selfish in the best way possible. By helping others in any way you can it's likely you're helping yourself in a significant way.

If you're still not convinced, look at the research conducted by Canadian social psychologist, Elizabeth Dunn, and Harvard Business School professor, Michael Norton.

Elizabeth's and Michael's book *Happy Money* is an amazing read about what science tells us about spending money to make us happy and is worth reading.

In fact, it might be the best few quid you've ever spent as

it's got the possibility of changing the way you perceive money to be useful as a contribution to more happiness and why you might not be spending as effectively as possible!

In *The Starbucks experiment* it was clearly shown that giving this card to someone else, as opposed to spending it on ourselves, made us happier.

It's a bit of a paradox, isn't it? We all know it's important to be kind to ourselves. There's been a recent trend in making sure we've all got enough 'me-time' and there's no denying that time spent on our own needs is really important.

However, time actually spent in service of others makes us happy too. I suppose, like most things in life, it's about balance.

You could certainly accuse me of oversimplification, as I appreciate that all of our lives are complicated. However, if we simply spent more time on doing the things we know made us happy and helping other people then we might have happier, healthier lives?

One of the main arguments against this gross over-simplification is always the same. It's time.

"Chris," you might be saying to yourself "I'm too busy doing other stuff to worry about this." I completely get it.

However, if the science is clear. We live happier, healthier, more fulfilled lives if we're kinder to ourselves and to others. There are things we waste time on that don't add value to our lives, social comparison, getting stuck in our own heads, procrastination and much more. Surely we should make an effort to take practical action to make more of an effort to be kinder to ourselves AND kinder to others.

Chapter 8
My perspective on kindness

When you think about kindness I'm certainly not what you expect. I'm not a positive psychologist like Ruth, or a daily practitioner of kindness like Bernadette. I don't use my time to deliver consistent kindness as effectively as Patrick or do as much for charity as Andy. I'm not an expert in philanthropy like Lauren and, while in my business I'm an advocate for 'doing well and doing good', I've got a lot to learn from many more people

I'm no Mother Theresa, Mahatma Ghandi or Fred Rogers. I'm just a man trying to be a better role model for his daughters and trying to understand what it means to be kind. To laugh more, to love more and to live a better life. A man whose desire to understand kindness started with a proud mum and a blue and white willow-patterned plate.

Looking back at all I've learned from interviewing people who are doing incredibly good work in the world and talking about kindness every week, there's a number of important things that stand out.

Firstly, kindness comes in many forms - from the smallest smile or words of encouragement to the ultimate grand gesture. We're all capable of kindness and we all have our own unique perspective on what it takes to be kind.

We hear about the elaborate charity challenges, the grand acts of good and the people who commit their lives to being permanent advocates of kindness. However, most of us aren't constantly focused on being kinder. Many of us, probably including you, lead complex, busy, messy lives and often we lose focus on doing good and helping our fellow man (or woman).

What we lose sight of is that kindness starts with being kinder to ourselves. Making sure that we're cutting ourselves some slack, ensuring we're grateful for what we've got, understanding that making mistakes is part of a natural process of learning.

- Being kind to ourselves is about looking at what we can control and worrying less about what we can't. Being kind to ourselves is making sure we fill our lives with positive influences.

- Being kind to ourselves is exercising despite having, like me, the reflexes of a baby giraffe.

- Being kind to ourselves is asking for help when we need it.

- Being kind to ourselves is also being kind to others.

What we sometimes forget is how simple being kind to others can be. It can be a simple thank you, a smile or compliment. It can be listening more and trying to be just a little more curious. It's trusting someone enough to actually ask for a favour or actively look for opportunities to help others or, perhaps, going on an adventure to deliver anonymous acts of kindness.

If we're looking for acts of kindness that take a tiny bit more time we can give blood, or share our knowledge and expertise for free in ways that will help the people who need it the most. Or, like Patrick Luong described, you might combine getting fit with doing good by joining an organisation like GoodGym. Alternatively, you could, through the power of technology, lend your eyes to someone sight-impaired to help make their day easier.

Another way you can improve your kindness game is to support causes you believe in. You can run, walk, climb or swing to raise money for a charity. We heard from Andy Furneaux, who talked about how all of the money raised by so many charities is used to actively support the members of our communities who need the most help.

There are so many amazing charities to support and you shouldn't find it difficult to find a cause you can really truly believe in. So my suggestion would be to actively tick things off your bucket list AND raise some money for an amazing cause.

However, that's not all. You could be like Danielle the Christmas Elf and roam the country supporting both charities and the people who use them, while having an adventure along the way!

There are also plenty of ways we can use our money for good. We can give our money to causes we believe in. Spend in ways that positively impact the world and ensure our buying decisions have a positive impact on the world. We can also start to think more carefully about how the wealth we accumulate has a positive impact on the world, and while there's no perfect way of doing this, think about how to use our wealth for good.

…and finally we can change our places of work to places where kindness thrives. Gone are the days of Gordon Gecko style competitiveness and a new modern spirit of business, which is more collaborative and supporting.

In the 80s and 90s greed might have been good, but in the 2020s collaboration and kindness in business is the way forward. However, while there are many different ways to run a business it's important to consider how and why our businesses can be kind. I'm not unique as a business leader in firmly believing you can do well AND do good.

We also talked to Rebecca Robbins about Project Aristotle, the research Google conducted that showed effective and efficient workplaces were built on a framework of 'Psychology Safety' – which encourages us to be empathetic, understanding and supportive in our workplaces.

What Google's research showed is that the kinder we are with the people we work with and the more this allowed us to feel supported and valued the more productive we become. So, whilst there are elements of the 80s I'd bring back in a minute - including kids TV, Rubik's cubes and Blackadder - the overarching business culture that promoted greed as good can stay in the past!

We also examined why it's important for businesses to be authentically kind and I've shared a few ideas on how businesses can exhibit kindness, including sponsorship, helping some people on a pro bono basis or providing a free service, Try to collaborate with people who are doing good in the world and sharing their knowledge to support others.

After all kindness is ultimately good for us. There's plenty of science telling us that being good to others, ultimately, improves our wellbeing - and if the science is telling us that simply being good to others generates amazing benefits for both our physical and mental health, who are we to argue?

However, I do recognise that whilst we might all understand the benefits of being a little bit kinder the journey towards being a bit better to others and ourselves isn't always a straightforward one.

Many of us know how paradoxical our behaviour can be at times and I believe the best recent example of how much of a paradox we humans are came from a musical theatre show about a politician over a century old.

I'm a massive fan of the hip hop musical Hamilton. I've been lucky enough to see the West End show and have recently rewatched the show on Disney +.

In case you haven't heard of Hamilton, (if you haven't where have you been?) it's a show about the first treasury secretary and one of the founding fathers of the United States of America.

While you may rather stick your head in a bucket than see a musical, let alone one about a long dead politician, something I reckon I would have said before actually seeing Hamilton, I'd humbly suggest that this work of genius is something you definitely don't want to miss.

As a story it's got everything - drama, conflict, love, peace, war and Hip Hop. It's literate and deep, but also maintains an incredible accessibility, which has led to Hamilton becoming an absolute smash hit. It certainly deserves a second, third, fourth and fifth watch. Then it's probably worth taking a break and then watching again. And again. And again.

There are plenty of lessons to learn from this particular story about one of the most interesting founding fathers. However, the biggest thing Hamilton reminded me of is how fundamentally flawed we are as humans.

The titular character is shown as a driven, but flawed, human being. A great man, and an incredibly sharp thinker, but not always a good man. The show is also full of the stories of the many individuals involved in the founding of the good 'ole US of A including Thomas Jefferson and George Washington. They are shown as virtuous, but often misguided, characters who are trying to achieve what they believe is right but nobody would suggest that Jefferson and Washington are perfect. For one thing, they purported to be advocates of freedom, but also continued to own slaves. However, despite their less savoury characteristics, it could be argued that they achieved great things.

Many of the characters in Hamilton are paradoxical in nature. They're great and awful. They're inspired and idiotic. They're loving and hateful. These characters show the best and worst of nature. The characters in this show, and the thing that makes this musical so amazing, is that the characters in Hamilton are deeply human.

Total evil or totally good people don't exist. We aren't entirely defined by what we spend our days doing, or whether we're parents or not, or what political party we choose to support or campaign for. We're complex. We're complicated. We're messy. Most of us are just trying to muddle through life in the best way we can, trying our best, but probably, in between all the times we get it right, we also get it wrong plenty of times along the way.

One of the things I think we could do to be kinder is to understand how imperfect we are, and also how fantastically complex and nuanced every single human being on the planet is and treat others with a little more respect of this fact. A little more forgiveness. A little more compassion.

The need for a little more compassion and forgiveness is as intense as it's ever been due to the way we often communicate online. Nuance and subtlety has been lost in a lot of online engagements and offense is taken, often when none is meant. It suits the particular social media platforms to drive this behaviour, suits the people who ply their trade through incendiary behaviour, but it does nothing for the majority of us who want to live happier and mentally healthier lives.

Seeing the world through the lens of every Twitter argument or forum free-for-all is a deeply depressing place and probably one of the reasons why my recent social media postings have either been photos of the Daems family days out, dodgy jokes, promotions for the podcast and really badly-timed Hamilton-related Tik Toks.

The internet is an amazing invention. One that has connected the world and created a wealth of opportunities than ever before. However, we've got to remember that behind any online interaction there's a real human. One that's as brilliant, but also as flawed, as all of us.

10% kinder

During 2020, while the world was fearful of the Coronavirus, Charlotte and I had the privilege of interviewing Melisa and Jaclyn who run the New York-based Kindness.org and are the authors of 'Be Kind'.

Kindness.org uses science to unlock the power and potential of humanity's greatest asset: kindness. As a research-led non-profit, its mission is to educate and inspire people to choose kindness first. Through their research hub, Kindlab they conduct scientific research to create products that help people measurably build a kinder world.

At the end of our interview I asked Melisa and Jaclyn a question about what their goal might be in ten years and Melissa has an insightful answer.

> *"It might be a longer term aspiration, Chris,*
> *but I'd like to see a world which is 10%*
> *kinder"*

This made me think - is it possible for all of us to be just

10% kinder? Could you spend 10% more time thinking about how you could be kinder to yourself? Spend some more time in acts of everyday kindness. Could you smile 10% more? Could you say thanks 10% more?

Could you increase the amount of time you give to acts of kindness by 10%? Could you give 10% more to charity? Could you think 10% harder about using your money for good or look at how you can improve the way you're kinder at work by 10%?

I'm pretty sure this is all possible and I hope this book is a catalyst for you to be a little bit kinder to yourself, to others, to the planet, with your money, with your time.

However, even if reading this is a catalyst to perform one tiny kind act more than you did yesterday it'll be worth it. Even if this book made you feel a tiny bit better it'll be worth it too.

The likelihood is that if you're reading this you're already pretty kind. So, do me a favour? Do something amazingly kind by sharing this book with someone you think might benefit from reading it. Hopefully, the stories in this book will help both you and also help spread the idea of kindness far and wide.

Looking back at the work we've done with *The Kindness Project* over the years I'm most proud that we've shared the stories of so many people doing amazingly good work in the world. However the reality is that I've got so much more out of this project than I've given.

In the early days of *The Kindness Project* I had the privilege of interviewing Chris Laney. Chris, as well as being one of the kindest most compassionate people I know, runs a business that does some amazing work in the community.

One of her particular projects was a reminiscence project,

funded by the National Lottery Heritage Fund. This project is designed to share the memories of people in the later years of life of their experiences of growing up in the east end of London in the first half of the twentieth century. Chris spent countless hours recording amazing tales of life gone by so that they could be saved for posterity.

After chatting to Chris about her project on the podcast I remember thinking about how much of an amazing audio legacy that particular project was. The grandchildren, great-grandchildren and great-great-grandchildren of the people interviewed could listen back for decades to come and hear the stories of their family, long since passed, in their own words.

As I write this it makes me think of the hours of *The Kindness Project* Charlotte and I have recorded. I wonder whether in decades to come, when I'm old and decrepit, whether Charlotte will find these recordings and share them with her future family.

I wonder whether she'll listen back and laugh at the funny, random and bizarre conversations we had. I wonder whether she'll chuckle at our chat about the conversation we had about stroking gorillas and even shed a tear at the podcast where we share the fondest stories of my mum at her best - something we did a few times when recording the podcast in the weeks just after my mum died.

I wonder if Charlotte's and Sophie's children, if they decide to go down the road of having their own families, will listen to the podcast. I wonder if their grand-children and future generations will too.

One unexpected consequence of hosting a podcast with your daughter is the audio legacy you create. You're sharing stories and creating memories we can listen back to for years to come and remember how much we enjoyed our time together.

Charlotte might choose not to do this. She might decide never to listen again. The podcasts in decades to come might be lost in the sands of time never to be listened to by my children, or their children, or the generations that follow. However, they might, and that gives me a feeling of satisfaction, an unexpected consequence of starting *The Kindness Project*.

We've managed to connect and speak to amazing people we'd never have met if hadn't had the podcast. People like Don Diffang, the London based scientist and founder of the kindness platform - *Do me a favour buddy*. The first time we met Don, he came to my office armed with free t-shirts for Charlotte and I with a simple slogan on the front;

"I helped the world suck a little less"

From that point I knew that Don was going to be someone who would make my life a bit better by knowing him. However he's not alone.

We've had loads of amazing guests, all of whom I've learned something from, all of whom are trying to do something positive in the world in their own unique way.

Some of them build amazing communities helping others to be kind, like the amazing Louise Baker who runs the *Postcards for kindness* Facebook group, which ensures that older people in care homes receive postcards from families traveling the world to combat loneliness and isolation.

Some of them promote the cause of kindness on our tellyboxes…like Leon Logothetis - host of the Netflix show - *The Kindness Diaries*.

Some of them do something both fun and meaningful, like Danielle Lazenby, who did a tour of the UK to deliver presents to children's hospices dressed as an elf.

Some help people through their work, not only the people who run amazing charities who have spoken to us, but also those who help support people improve their wellbeing.

There's loads more, many of whom are mentioned all through this book, who believe in the power of kindness and use that power every single day. For those who I've mentioned in this book and all of those who I haven't, I thank you equally for sharing your stories with me. You've helped me become a little more knowledgeable, a little kinder, a little more curious and a little more hopeful that most people are good, and there's a significant amount who are amazing.

I also hope that if you haven't listened to the podcast that you find the time to listen to some of the amazing people we've been lucky enough to interview.

I hope it's been a catalyst for you to be kinder to yourself or supported you to perform small acts of kindness every single day.

I hope you've donated either a little bit of time, a little bit of money or a little bit of both to an amazing cause. I hope you've used your money for good and you've managed to become a little kinder in your workplace. I hope you pass this book on to, or buy a copy for, someone who could benefit from reading it.

As for Charlotte and I we're still on a mission to get a bit better. I'm still far from perfect, but I know that *The Kindness Project* has made me a better listener, a better dad and a better man.

I'm not convinced I'm a 10% kinder person yet, but hopefully I'm on my way there. I hope you become a little bit kinder each and every day.

After all,

What would the world look like if we were all 10% kinder?